INVESTOR'S
TAX SAVINGS
GUIDE

Jack Crestol, CPA, LLM

and

Warren G. Wintrub, CPA, JD

LYBRAND, ROSS BROS. & MONTGOMERY

Herman M. Schneider, CPA, LLM

EASTMAN DILLON, UNION SECURITIES & CO.

DOW JONES BOOKS
PRINCETON, NEW JERSEY

CONTENTS

II. PRINCIPLES OF TAXATION OF SECURITIES TRANSACTIONS

PREFACE

The investor's primary objective in investing in securities is to make a profit: buy low, sell high. Unfortunately, however, getting the *most* profit from a year's security transactions is not a simple matter of buying low and selling high, because the tax laws determine how much of the profit can be kept.

The informed investor measures his economic gain or yield in terms of after-tax dollars or the amount of additional cash available after considering all expenses including income taxes. It should be emphasized, however, that although the informed investor should be highly conscious of tax factors, he will rarely allow these tax factors to affect an economic decision. A short-term gain taxed at ordinary rates is still superior to a long-term capital loss, no matter how heavily the gain is taxed.

To aid investors in their understanding of how security transactions are taxed and the kind of planning measures necessary to maximize net gain, this book was first issued in 1966 and revised in 1967. It has again been thoroughly revised to reflect new developments including the Tax Reform Act of 1969, and now provides in Part I a guide to tax-savings opportunities, and in Part II a summary of the tax rules an investor needs to know to plan effectively. This guide is not intended to show investors how to realize economic gains in securities transactions, but rather how to obtain the best tax advantages in recognizing gains or losses. To this end, tax savings opportunities are discussed in the form of objectives, such as postponing tax recognition of gain, converting short-term gains into long-term gains, etc. For example, the investor may be able to create a long-term gain and an approximately equivalent short-term loss in the same or different years by acquiring a commodity straddle (the purchase and short sale of the same commodity future calling for delivery in different months), while at the same time achieving his intended economic objectives.

The provisions of the 1969 Tax Reform Act will have only a minor effect on the average investor. It was intended to apply principally to high-tax bracket individuals who paid relatively little or no tax on their substantial incomes. The principal changes affecting investors are (i) the inclusion of one-half the long-term capital gains in the computation of the 10 percent minimum tax, (ii) the restrictions placed on excess investment interest expense, (iii) the increased capital gains tax on long-term capital gains exceeding $50,000, (iv) the inclusion of long-term capital gains in income averaging, and (v) the 50 percent reduction of long-term capital losses applied against ordinary income. These and other provisions will be discussed in detail in the text. The interplay among the various provisions will make tax planning even more meaningful.

This book is concerned with the Federal tax liabilities of an individual U.S. resident investor who files his income tax return on the cash basis. Although many of the ideas presented and the discussion of the relevant income tax provisions may also apply (with or without some modification) to non-resident aliens, traders, dealers, partnerships, trusts, estates and corporations, the text does not consider such possible application. In addition, the discussion is confined to transactions in securities of publicly-held corporations and does not consider the special tax provisions relating to closely-held or related corporations. In all the examples, it is assumed that the investor files his tax return on the calendar year basis. Furthermore, for the sake of simplicity, a capital gains tax rate of 25 percent is used and the effect of the tax surcharge is ignored in these examples. Unless otherwise indicated, all examples are applicable under the 1969 Tax Reform Act.

For practical reasons, State and local tax liabilities are not considered herein. Such liabilities are usually small in relation to Federal tax liabilities and are frequently computed on comparable bases. The investor is warned, however, that situations may arise where State or local tax liabilities may be large enough to influence an investor's tax planning. Each investor should acquaint himself with the nature and magnitude of such taxes as they apply to him.

For the convenience of the reader, the discussion of tax savings opportunities is cross-referenced to the discussion of tax principles, official authorities are referred to in footnotes and indexed in the appendix, and a detailed table of contents is provided. Many readers will prefer first to scan the tax savings opportunities for interesting suggestions and then to read the sections of Part II that apply.

———

The authors wish to acknowledge their appreciation of the invaluable assistance of their associates in the offices of Lybrand, Ross Bros. & Montgomery. In particular, Norman E. Auerbach, CPA, James B. Fish, Jr., CPA, Joseph M. Lobel, Sheldon Rabinowitz, CPA, Anthony P. Rua, CPA, and Godfrey W. Welsch, CPA, assisted in preparation of the earlier editions and/or this revision.

Jack Crestol
Herman M. Schneider
Warren G. Wintrub

New York, N.Y.

TAX SAVINGS OPPORTUNITIES

INTRODUCTION

The ideas discussed in this section are intended to present the investor with alternative legitimate methods of casting a transaction so that the investor can either reduce his tax liability or defer the tax to another year. Many of these ideas have been sanctioned by court decisions or by Treasury regulations or rulings. However, the investor should be aware that the Treasury may attack new areas on various grounds, sometimes despite court approval of the transaction.

POSTPONE TAX RECOGNITION OF GAIN OR LOSS

The transactions discussed below will postpone the recognition of the gain or loss, but will not change the character of the gain or loss when recognized for tax purposes. Several of the ideas have general application, while others are limited to specific types of investments.

"Short Against the Box"

An investor can sell a security but defer the recognition of gain until the next year by selling short an equal number of shares and covering the short sale in the following year with the shares originally held. This is commonly known as "selling short against the box." The long-term or short-term nature of the gain will be determined at the time of the short sale and therefore will not be affected by the deferral. The amount of the tax will depend on the taxpayer's other income and the tax rates in effect in the year in which the gain is recognized. Deferral of the gain, therefore, may result in a higher or lower effective tax rate on the gain, and should be taken into account in determining whether or not to go short against the box.

1

Example: An investor may wish to protect his profit in stock acquired on May 1, 1970 for $20 per share, and which is selling on December 1, 1970 for $50. Instead of recognizing a $30 per share long-term capital gain in 1970, the investor could sell short the stock at $50 and defer the closing of such sale until January of 1971, at which time the long-term gain of $30 per share (less transfer fees and taxes) will be recognized. If the stock was acquired on July 1, 1970, so that the holding period of the stock was not more than six months at the time of the short sale, the gain recognized upon the closing of the short sale would be a short-term capital gain. (See discussion of short sales, pages 48 to 53.)

The short sale may also be used to sell a depreciated security but defer the recognition of the loss until the next year. Ordinarily it is more advantageous to deduct the loss in the current year. However, under certain circumstances, it may be more beneficial taxwise to postpone recognizing the loss. The following are some examples where the losses should be postponed.

Example (a): *Excess deductions:* T's deductions exceed his income, including $3,000 of capital gains, by $5,000. On December 1, T wants to sell a stock and realize a capital loss of $2,000. There would be no tax benefit if the capital loss is recognized in the current year because there is no taxable income and the excess deductions cannot be carried to another year. (See page 27.) A short sale of the stock will enable T to apply the capital loss against his income in the year the sale is closed.

Example (b): *Long-term loss and short-term gain:* In 1970, T has realized $5,000 of short-term gains and $5,000 of long-term losses. He expects to realize short-term gains and long-term gains in 1971. T has suffered a $4,000 loss on a stock acquired late in 1970 and wants to sell it before there is a further drop in its value. By selling the stock short and closing it early in 1971, T can offset his 1970 long-term losses against his short-term gains and offset the postponed $4,000 short-term loss against his 1971 short-term gains. If he recognized the loss in 1970, the loss would be applied against his 1970 short-term gains. However, only $1,000 of the $5,000 long-term loss could be offset against the remaining 1970 short-term gains, $2,000 of the loss would be applied against $1,000 of his 1970 ordinary income (see page 35) and $2,000 of the long-term loss would be offset against 1971 long-term gains. T would obtain an additional $1,000 deduction in 1970, but at the expense of having $4,000 more of short-term gains in 1971 and only a $2,000 reduction in long-term gains.

Example (c): *Income averaging:* As a result of the new income averaging rules (see page 78), T can pay the minimum tax on his capital gains in 1970. T expects short-term gains in 1971 and expects to pay a much larger tax on his 1971 gains. T has incurred a $5,000 loss on a security and wants to sell it before there is a further decline. By selling short in 1970 and closing in 1971, T can obtain a greater tax benefit from the loss.

Example (d): *Maximum tax on earned income:* T's annual salary is $100,000. His tax preference items ordinarily are less than $30,000, but in 1971 he expects to exercise qualified stock options which will increase his total tax preference items by $25,000. (See page 77.) He has an unrealized loss on a stock of $10,000 which he can apply against his capital gains in 1970 or 1971. By selling short in 1970 and covering in 1971, T can increase the amount of wages that will be subject to a maximum tax of 60 percent rather than 70 percent. By deferring the loss, T will have a greater tax for 1970, but there will be a substantial decrease in tax for the two-year period.

Under certain circumstances, the broker may release to the investor a substantial portion of the funds arising from the short sale or allow the purchase of other securities with the purchasing power created because of such short sale. Interest will ordinarily be charged on the short sale. The investor should determine the position of his broker in this situation before making the short sale. It may be possible to keep both positions open for a long period of time, have the use of the funds or additional purchasing power during this period, and still avoid recognition of gain.

The investor can defer the recognition of any gain on his stock and still *Acquisition* minimize the possible reduction in the amount of his gain by acquiring *of a Put* an option to sell the stock (a "Put"). The advantage of this method as compared to the use of a short sale, as discussed above, is that in the event the stock continues to rise, the investor obtains the benefit of such rise. However, the cost of acquiring this insurance against decline is normally in the area of 10 to 15 percent of the value of the underlying security. This varies in accordance with the period of time that the option will run, the volatility of the stock and supply and demand for the

Put. A tax disadvantage under either method is that if the underlying security is held less than six months at the time of the short sale or acquisition of the Put, any gain on subsequent sale will generally be treated as short-term, since the holding period of the stock will not begin until the short sale is covered or the Put is exercised, expires or is disposed of. (See discussion of short sales on page 50.)

Example: Assume that in the last part of the previous example where the investor owned stock acquired July 1, 1970 at $20 per share, he purchased on December 1, 1970 a six month, 10 day Put at $50 for the equivalent of $5 per share. The investor then has the right to "put" or sell the stock to the writer of the option at any time during the period for $50 per share, regardless of the then selling price of the stock. If the market value of the stock rises, for example, to $75 per share and the investor wishes to close out the transaction, he can sell the stock in the open market, recognizing a $55 per share, short-term capital gain (the stock was held for less than six months at the time the Put was acquired). He would try to sell the Put prior to the end of the six-month period, realizing a short-term loss of approximately $5 per share, in lieu of merely letting the Put expire, in which case the loss would be long-term.

If the investor had sold short the stock at $50 per share in lieu of acquiring the Put, he would have limited his gain to $30 per share. Thus, for a cost of approximately $5 per share, the Put insures a minimum gain and allows potentially substantial gain possibilities for the six-month period in the event of a rise in the stock market.

If the market value of the stock should fall, for example, to $30 per share by June 2, 1970 (Put held for more than six months), he would sell the Put for the equivalent price of approximately $20 per share ($50 option price less market value of stock of $30) and, therefore, recognize long-term gain of approximately $15 per share ($20 per share proceeds less $5 per share cost of the Put). The stock would then be sold for $30, resulting in a capital gain of $10 per share which is given *short-term* treatment even though the stock was held for more than six months. This occurs with respect to the gain because at the time of the acquisition of the Put, such shares were held for less than six months, thus bringing in effect the short sale rules. If the stock were instead sold for $15 per share, a *loss* of $5 per share would be treated as *long-term*, since the short sale rules would not be applicable.

A discussion of the seller's option is to be found on page 11. Selling via this route will enable the seller to take advantage of the current market price and still defer recognition of gain and add up to 60 days to his holding period. Thus, a seller who has held a security for from four to six months can convert a short-term gain into a long-term gain without further exposure to market risk.

Deferred Delivery under New York Stock Exchange Rule 64(3) (Seller's Option)

A cash-basis investor selling stock toward the end of his taxable year may control which year the gain is to be recognized. When stock is sold in the "regular way," as is the case in most instances, the settlement day will be the fifth business day following the trade date. A loss will be recognized in the year in which the trade date falls, but a profit is not taxable until the subsequent year in which the settlement date falls. The cash-basis investor may cause the gain to be recognized in the year of the trade by making the sale "for cash." (See page 11 dealing with deferred delivery under N.Y. Stock Exchange Rule 64(3) for possible postponement of gain for up to 60 days.)

Year-End Sales

The following table illustrates these rules:

Examples of Tax Recognition of Year-End Sales

Stock	Cost	Selling Amount	Gain (Loss)	Date of Sale	Terms	Year Transaction Recognized for Tax Purposes
A	$10	$15	$5	12/28/70	Regular way	1971
B	10	15	5	12/28/70	For cash	1970
C	10	5	(5)	12/28/70	Regular way	1970
D	10	15	5	11/15/70	Deferred delivery (seller's option) — 60 days	1971

An investor who has a large security position with substantial unrealized appreciation and who is negotiating a sale thereof in a private transaction with payment to be spread over a period of years, should consider the availability of the installment sales election of reporting the income realized as a way of deferring the payment of the capital gains tax. Payments in the year of sale must not exceed 30 percent of the selling price. The contract should provide for a minimum of four percent annual interest in order to avoid the imputed interest tax provision. Some tender offers, where debt obligations are issued, have been ar-

Installment Sale of Securities in a Private Transaction

ranged so as to enable the seller to elect the installment method of reporting the gain. Note, however, that under the Tax Reform Act certain demand obligations or readily tradeable obligations received in corporate acquisitions are treated as cash payments. (See page 65.)

Exchange of Bonds Holders of certain U.S. Government bonds may have an opportunity to exchange such bonds for other governmental obligations without recognition of gain. The conversion of Series "E" bonds into other government obligations has the effect of deferring the interest element until disposition or redemption of the new bonds. Tax-free exchanges of other types of bonds are also permitted. (See page 65 for discussion dealing with exchange of bonds.)

Contribution or Bargain Sale of Securities A taxpayer can permanently avoid recognition of gain on appreciated securities by giving them to a charity or can substantially avoid tax on the appreciation by selling them to a charity for a price equal to his basis. The charitable contribution deduction in the former situation is the market value, and in the latter case is the difference between market value and the selling price. Although a bargain sale to charity after December 19, 1969 is subject to tax (see page 30), except for some top-bracketed taxpayers, a bargain sale generally will result in greater after-tax dollars to the donor as demonstrated by the following illustration:

Comparison of Direct Contribution with Bargain Sales

	Direct Contribution	Bargain Sale at Cost
Value of Property $1,000		
Tax Basis 400		
Sales Proceeds	$ —	$400
Tax (at 25%)	—	60
Contribution	1,000	600
Tax Savings (50% bracket)	500	300
After-tax dollars retained	500	640

INSURE PROPER TIMING AND NATURE OF GAIN OR LOSS

An investor may be in a current security position where some positive action on his part will assure him the desired tax result.

Nature and Timing of Capital Losses Investors should consider taking capital losses within the six-month, short-term period in order to have the loss sustained carried forward as a short-term loss. Long-term losses sustained are carried forward as long-term losses in succeeding years and must first offset long-term gains in the year to which carried before offsetting short-term gains. (See discussion of capital loss carry-overs on page 35.) It is important where possible to arrange the year's transactions so that long-term losses are deductible against short-term gains. To the extent that a capital loss offsets a long-term gain, the average investor is reducing income tax at only an effective *maximum* rate of 25 to 35 percent. However, through the interplay of the 10 percent minimum tax and the maximum tax on earned income provisions the maximum effective rate on long-term gains may exceed 50 percent for certain investors. (See page 77.)

Example:

	1	2	3	4
Current year long-term gain	$10,000	$10,000	$10,000	—
Current year short-term gain	10,000	10,000	10,000	$10,000
Loss carry-over long-term	—	(10,000)	—	(10,000)
Loss carry-over short-term	—	—	(10,000)	—
Net long-term gain	10,000	—	10,000	—
Net short-term gain	10,000	10,000	—	—
Tax (assume 50% bracket)	$ 7,500	$ 5,000	$ 2,500	—

Tax savings on $10,000 long-term capital loss carry-over (compare Column 1 with Column 2) is $2,500. If the loss carry-over was short-term, such savings would have been $5,000 (compare Column 1 with Column 3). The same savings can be achieved from a long-term loss carry-over (Column 4) only if there are sufficient short-term gains and no long-term gains in the year.

Where part of a position in securities is sold or transferred, adequate identification should be made so as to assure proper and desired tax consequences. (See page 42.) **Identification of Securities**

Example:
Position in XYZ Co.:

Date Purchased	Shares	Basis
January 5, 1965	100	$1,000
March 10, 1967	100	3,300
March 15, 1970	100	1,500
September 30, 1970	100	2,800

On December 15, 1970, the investor sells 100 shares for $3,000. By identifying the shares sold, he will recognize either long-term gain (against purchase 1/5/65 or 3/15/70), short-term gain (against purchase 9/30/70) or long-term loss against purchase 3/10/67). The choice is his. Without proper identification of the certificates delivered, the stock from the 1/5/65 purchase will be deemed the 100 shares sold. (See page 42.)

Worthless Securities —When and How to Take a Loss
It is frequently difficult to establish the worthlessness of a security in order to obtain a deduction. Generally, a sale for more than a nominal amount will show that worthlessness did not occur in an earlier year barred by the statute of limitations for refunds. Where the year of worthlessness is in doubt, protective claims for refunds should be filed for each possible year. (See page 66.)

Create Wash Sales
Under certain circumstances it may be desirable to create a wash sale so as to add back to the basis of the newly acquired security, the disallowed loss and holding period. This might be the case where the investor, within 30 days after the sale of securities at a loss, realizes the disadvantageous timing of the capital transactions. (See discussion of Wash Sale Rules, page 44.)

> *Example:* T, after holding ABC stock for 5½ months, liquidates his position to realize a short-term loss. Subsequently, but within the next 30 days, ABC stock suddenly starts to rise. T now feels that ABC stock has potential appreciation. By repurchasing ABC stock within 30 days after the previous sale, under the wash sale provisions, his loss is not recognized for tax purposes and instead such loss would increase the basis of the new shares acquired. What is more important is that the ABC stock will start off with a 5½ month holding period, thus according sudden substantial overall gain, long-term capital gain treatment by merely holding ABC stock for an additional one-half month period.

Another instance where it might be desirable to create a wash sale can be illustrated by the following:

> *Example:* T, on May 1, 1970 purchased 100 shares of ABC stock at $100 per share (Lot 1) and five months later on October 1, 1970 purchased an additional 100 shares at $70 per share (Lot 2). By October 20, 1970, ABC has substantially appreciated in value and is selling at $95 per share. If T sells the 200 shares of ABC at $95 per share, he will recognize a net short-term gain of $2,000 ($2,500 gain on Lot 2 less $500 loss on Lot 1).

8

If instead, T sold on October 20, 1970 100 shares (Lot 1), the $500 loss sustained is not recognized for tax purposes since T acquired 100 shares of ABC stock (Lot 2) within 30 days prior to such sale. Thus, the $500 loss would increase to $7,500 the basis of the 100 shares acquired on October 1, 1970. More relevant is the new holding period of the remaining 100 shares of ABC stock. The 5 month, 19 day holding period of the Lot 1 shares is added to the 19 day holding period of the Lot 2 100 shares. Thus, for tax purposes, the remaining 100 shares of ABC stock are deemed to have been held for more than six months and a sale of such shares on the next day, October 21, 1970, for $9,500 will result in the $2,000 net gain being treated as long-term.[1]

Commodity Futures— Create Gain and Loss in Different Taxable Years

Futures in the same commodity but with different delivery dates are not subject to the short sale rules. Thus, a taxpayer can buy and short sell the same commodity with different delivery dates and create capital gains and losses in different years. (See page 13.)

Obligations Issued at a Discount

An investor may elect in any taxable year to include in income annually the increase in the redemption value of certain non-interest bearing obligations issued at a discount, such as Series "E" savings bonds. Thus, if it is advantageous to increase income of a given year, the election can be made. If an election is not made during his lifetime, it can be made on the deceased investor's final return. (See page 26.)

CONVERT SHORT-TERM GAIN INTO LONG-TERM GAIN

Investors owning appreciated securities or options for less than six months may wish to protect their economic gain and still maintain their position for more than six months in order to have the recognized gain treated as long-term. The ensuing transactions may accomplish this objective. In addition a suggestion is given as to how to dispose of appreciated positions in "when-issued" contracts held for more than six months so that the gain recognized will be long-term instead of short-term.

[1] Code: 1223(4)

Sale of Call on Appreciated Long Position

An investor who has owned appreciated stock for less than six months can sell a Call on the stock which will not expire until the stock has been held for more than six months. The investor will thus give the purchaser of the Call an option to acquire the investor's stock at a specific price within a specified period of time. If the stock should have a further moderate increase in value, and the Call is exercised toward the end of its term, the investor will be assured of long-term capital gain to the extent that the Call price plus the amount received on the sale of the Call exceeds the basis of the stock. If the stock has substantially increased in value, the investor could buy other shares of the stock in the open market to deliver against the Call, recognizing a short-term loss, and sell his long position for greater long-term gain.

> *Example:* T acquires 100 shares of ABC on 2/1/70 at $10 per share. On 6/5/70 ABC is selling at $30 per share. T sells a 60-day Call at $30 for the equivalent of $2 per share ($200). If the ABC stock is selling after 8/1/70 at slightly above $30, the holder of the Call will exercise it and T will recognize a long-term capital gain of $22 per share ($30 plus $2 less $10). If ABC stock is selling at $40, T would buy 100 new shares of ABC at $40, and sell them to the holder of the Call at $30, thus recognizing a short-term capital loss of $8 per share. He could also sell his long position with a basis of $10 for $40, recognizing a long-term gain of $30. His net economic gain is still $22, but $30 is long-term gain and $8 is short-term loss.

If the market value of the stock should fall, the investor is economically protected to the extent of the premium received on the Call, which would be taxed as ordinary income if not exercised. Under the facts in the example, an investor in the 50 percent tax bracket will realize greater economic gain after taxes by waiting for a more than six-month holding period before selling, provided that ABC stock stays above $22 (long-term gain of at least $12 netting $9 plus $1 of after-tax income on $2 proceeds from the sale of the Call is equivalent to the $20 of short-term gain which would have been realized from a sale at $30). Thus unless there is a substantial break in the market, the investor will be assured of some long-term capital gain with a hedge against a decline to the extent of the premium received on the sale of the Call.

If the Call is sold initially at a price below the market, the investor will increase the chances that the Call will be exercised, so that the increased premium for writing the more valuable Call will be given long-term capital gain treatment. However, the demand for such a Call is limited, and consequently the amount of premium received aside from the intrinsic value of the Call because of the lower Call price, will be reduced.

The investor may take advantage of the current market price and still prolong his holding period for up to 60 days. This is accomplished by selling at today's market price, and contracting that payment and delivery will take place on a specified date within 60 days following the date of contract, with all dividends to stockholders of record before the delivery date belonging to the seller. Special arrangements must be made to have the dividends accrue to the seller. Otherwise under the normal deferred delivery transaction, dividends payable after the contract date would go to the buyer which might affect the rule as to when the sale takes place. The intent of the parties is that title passes on the delivery date. Thus an investor who has a holding period of between four and six months could convert unrealized short-term gain into long-term gain without any economic risk. It is understood that the Treasury's position in such a case is that the contract date is not regarded as controlling, and that the sale does not take place until the delivery date. A slight reduction in sales price is generally required to obtain a purchaser for deferred delivery stock.

Deferred Delivery under NYSE Rule 64(3) (Seller's Option)

> *Example:* T acquired XYZ stock on August 1, 1970 at $30 per share. On December 15, 1970 the market value has risen to $64 at which time T wishes to liquidate his position and thereby protect his gain. By selling on a deferred delivery basis, for delivery on February 2, 1971, usually at a $1 to $2 discount (assuming no usual dividend record date falls in the interim), T will recognize in 1971 long-term gain of approximately $32 per share ($62 discounted selling price less $30 cost) in lieu of recognizing $34 short-term gain per share in 1970. T, who is in the 50 percent tax bracket, will earn in after-tax dollars, $24 per share under the deferred delivery sale, in lieu of $17 per share had he sold the stock in the regular way on December 15, 1970.

Where an investor has held an appreciated six-month, ten-day Call for less than six months, he may economically protect himself against a decline in the market by selling short a comparable number of shares of the underlying stock. If after the six-month holding period the Call is still appreciated, he can sell the Call, recognizing long-term gain, and close out the short sale, recognizing short-term gain or loss. In the event the market continues to rise, a sale of the Call after the six-month

Selling Short Against Appreciated Calls to Insure Gain

11

holding period will result in an increased long-term capital gain and the closing of the short position would create a short-term loss. In any event the investor has locked in his economic profit. The Call and the underlying stock are not considered substantially identical so as to come within the short sale rules.[2] (See page 51.)

> *Example:* T acquires on March 1, 1970 a six-month, ten-day Call on 100 shares of ABC stock at $30 per share for a cost of $400. On June 1, 1970, ABC stock is selling at $50. By selling short 100 shares at $50, T is assured of economic gain of at least $1,600 ($5,000 short sale amount less a cost of $3,000 for the stock if purchased and $400 for the Call). Assume that on September 2, 1970, ABC stock is selling at $70. T would sell the Call for approximately $4,000 (difference between market value of $70 per share and the Call price of $30 per share), recognizing $3,600 of long-term gain (after deducting cost of $400 for the Call). T would sustain a short-term loss of $2,000 on the closing of the short sale. His economic pre-tax gain is still $1,600. If the ABC stock had instead been selling at $15 on September 2, T would realize $3,500 short-term gain on the closing of the short sale, a long-term loss of $400 on the expiration of the Call (loss would be short-term if the Call was sold prior to the six-month holding period), or a net economic gain of $3,100.

CREATE LONG-TERM GAIN AND SHORT-TERM LOSS

Arbitraging Securities Not Substantially Identical

Long-term capital gains can be obtained in arbitrage situations if the long position is held open for more than six months and if the securities sold short are not "substantially identical" to the long securities for purposes of the short sale rules. (See page 51.)

> *Example:* X and Y corporations plan to merge and the stock of X corporation will be exchanged evenly for shares of Y corporation. Prior to approval by the shareholders, the two securities are not considered to be substantially identical. (See page 51.) X stock is selling at $20 and Y stock is selling at $22. The investor buys X stock and sells Y stock short. It is immaterial that the X stock subsequently becomes "substantially identical" to the Y stock.[3] It should also be immaterial that after an

---

[2] Rev. Rul. 58-384, C.B. 1958-2, 410   [3] Rev. Rul. 62-153, C.B. 1962-2, 186

exchange for X stock, Y stock is now held in a long position. The exchange should not be deemed an acquisition of the Y stock bringing into play the short sale rules. (See page 48.)

The closing of the long position of the Y stock received in the exchange against the short position of Y after the requisite six-month holding period will result in long-term gain to the extent of the initial spread of $2 per share. If the value of Y stock at the time of delivery rises above $22 per share, then the Y stock received on the exchange should be sold in order to recognize long-term capital gains greater than the initial spread of $2 per share. The short position should be covered through the purchase in the open market of Y stock, resulting in the recognition of a short-term capital loss which could be utilized to offset short-term capital gains. The net economic gain will be equal to the initial spread of $2 per share, but the character of the gain and loss for tax purposes will be different.

Commodity Futures

The purchase and short sale of the same commodity future calling for delivery in different months are not within the short sale rules. (See page 48.) The investor may avail himself of this statutory exception, when entering into this transaction for profit, to establish a long-term gain and an approximately equivalent short-term loss, where such is desired. In addition, the investor may create capital gains and losses in different years so as to offset unwanted capital gains or losses previously realized during the year.

Example (*a*): *Long-term gain and short-term loss:* On June 1, 1970 T enters into a contract to buy 10,000 ounces of May 1971 silver and at the same time enters into a contract to sell 10,000 ounces of March 1971 silver. More than six months later, on December 2, 1970, assume both futures have risen in value by 50 cents an ounce. T, by closing each contract out separately, will realize a long-term capital gain of $5,000 on the long position of May 1971 silver and a $5,000 short-term capital loss on the short sale of March 1971 silver. (Gain or loss recognized on the closing of a short position in commodity futures will always be short-term no matter how long the position is kept open.) The market price of futures having different maturity dates will not necessarily fluctuate proportionately. However, the proportionate fluctuations in prices tend to be closer as the maturity dates are more distant in time. A careful study must be made of the particular commodity future to be used in the transaction to determine the possibilities of economic gain or loss. It is possible that the transaction may result in an economic loss which could outweigh the tax advantage.

If both futures have declined in value, T should close out the long position before his holding period is more than six months in order to prevent the loss from becoming long-term. The closing of both contracts prior to such six-month holding period, except for differences in fluctuations of price, will result in almost a complete wash of gain and loss, both being short-term.

Example (b): *Create capital gains and losses in different years:* T has large short-term gains realized in the current taxable year. The use of commodity futures will enable him to recognize loss in one year, with comparable gain in the next year, and be subjected to little market risk.

T could enter into the transaction described in (a) above in November of 1970. Assume that the market value of silver rises in value by 50 cents an ounce, then T would close out his short position in March 1971 silver by December 31, 1970, recognizing a short-term loss of $5,000.

He immediately would sell short July 1971 silver in order to be protected against a decline of silver futures. In the subsequent year, both the May 1971 long position and July 1971 short position would be sold with a resulting net short-term gain approximately equivalent to the $5,000 short-term loss recognized in December 1970. Similar action on the part of T in case of market decline will accomplish the same results.

It is possible under the transactions described in (a) and (b) above to defer paying a tax on the short-term gains realized in the earlier year and also convert the gains into long-term gains in the succeeding year provided there is a rise in the market value of the future and there is sufficient time left before the maturity dates of the contracts to accomplish the latter objective.

Acquisition of Shares in a Mutual Fund

An investor in a high tax bracket and having large short-term capital gains would welcome the opportunity to create short-term capital losses and long-term capital gains, and thereby convert his realized short-term capital gains into long-term capital gains. The investor should consider buying shares in a mutual fund immediately prior to a large capital gain distribution, hold the mutual fund for more than

14

31 days and then liquidate his position.[4] The market value of the fund will drop approximately equivalent to the amount of the capital gain distribution if there is no other change in the value of the assets of the fund for the 31-day period. The investor will treat the capital gains distribution as long-term and the loss on the sale of the fund as short-term. However, the investor is subjected to the vagaries of the market for the 31-day period. The "loading" charges of some mutual funds would increase the loss on the sale to such an extent as to make this device uneconomic. However, shares of so-called "no-load" funds may be available. Shares of a "close-end" mutual fund could also be utilized in a similar manner; however, a commission expense will be incurred upon acquisition and subsequent sale of such shares.

> *Example:* T purchases on November 15, 1970, 1,000 shares of ABC Fund (a no-load fund) for $20 per share. ABC Fund distributes a $2 long-term capital gain dividend. T will recognize long-term capital gains on the receipt of the $2,000 distribution even though he has held ABC stock for merely one day. The value of ABC Fund will fall to $18 per share. Assuming that there are no changes in the value of ABC Fund for the next 31 days, T would sell the 1,000 shares after December 16, 1970 and realize a $2,000 short-term capital loss (cost of $20,000 less selling amount of $18,000).

CREATE CAPITAL GAIN AND ORDINARY DEDUCTION

Selling Short before Ex-Dividend Date

An investor intending to establish a short position should enter into the short sale before the ex-dividend date in order to obtain an ordinary deduction for the amount paid as a dividend on the short sale and thus have the resulting equivalent amount potentially available as capital gain. (However, if the dividend is a stock dividend or liquidating dividend, the Treasury will not allow the deduction.) Generally the market value of the stock on the ex-dividend date falls in an amount equal to the dividend paid. If the investor subsequently covers his short position and there is no other variation in the value of the stock, he will realize a short-term capital gain approximately equivalent to the amount paid as a dividend on the short sale. A short-term gain might be desired in order to offset short-term losses that would otherwise offset long-term

---

[4] Code section 852(b)(4) necessitates a 31-day holding period; otherwise the loss on sales of the stock would be treated as long-term.

15

gains. However, it should be noted that where the sole purpose of the transaction is tax avoidance, the deductibility of the dividend paid may be questioned. (See page 69.)

> *Example:* ABC stock is scheduled to go ex-dividend a $1 dividend on December 15, 1970; T wishes to sell the stock short at $60. If he establishes the short position prior to December 15, 1970, he will have to pay $1 per share for such dividend, for which he becomes entitled to a $1 per share ordinary deduction. Assuming no other changes in market value, ABC stock should fall in price to $59 thereby creating a potential short-term gain of $1 per share. However, if T waits until December 15, 1970 he will establish his short position at a price of $59 per share, the market value on that day. T will not have any ordinary deduction, nor the built-in potential capital gain of $1 per share.

Sale and Repurchase of Appreciated Bonds

Holders of taxable bonds which are selling at a premium and have appreciated in value, for example, because of changes in the going interest rate, should sell the bonds, and immediately repurchase an equal number of the same bonds. Gains on the sale of the bonds held for more than six months are taxed at the lower capital gains rate. The premium paid on the subsequent repurchase (not attributable to any conversion privilege) may be deducted against ordinary income through amortization usually computed to the maturity date.[5] (See page 62.)

> *Example:* T owns $50,000 of 6% noncallable and nonconvertible XYZ bonds due January 1, 1975 which he acquired at par in 1966. These bonds on January 2, 1970 are selling at 105 and are therefore worth $52,500. If T sells these bonds, he will recognize a long-term capital gain of $2,500. Assuming he still wants to maintain his investment position in these bonds, he would repurchase them at 105 for $52,500. T should then elect to amortize the $2,500 premium over the remaining term of the bonds. Thus T would be entitled to a deduction against ordinary income of $500 per year ($2,500 amortized over the period of 1970 through 1975). T, in the 50

---

[5] Rev. Rul. 55-353, C.B. 1955-1, 381

percent tax bracket, may pay a capital gain tax of $625 in 1970, but would have available ordinary deductions each year which might result in tax savings of $250 annually or $1,250 over the five-year period.

With interest rates at currently high levels, many high grade low interest rate bonds are selling at substantial discounts. Investors who anticipate a decline in the interest rates are in a position to make substantial gains by purchasing these deep discount bonds on the highest margin available. The interest income on these bonds is taxable at ordinary income rates, but the spread between the purchase price and the amount received on sale or redemption is taxed at capital gain rates. The interest paid on the bank loans is deductible (see page 68 for discussion of Tax Reform Act restrictions on investment interest expense) against ordinary income. This type of transaction is even more attractive if the interest expense is prepaid, but the Treasury has limited the prepayment to a one-year period.[6] Moreover, the higher the income tax bracket of the investor, the greater will be his after-tax gain.

Deep Discount Bonds

> *Example:* T, in the 50 percent bracket, purchases on February 1, 1970, $100,000 of XYZ 4% bonds due February 1, 1975 at 80, which is financed by a bank loan for $80,000 at 9 percent interest. Assuming the bonds are redeemed at par at maturity, the following are the pre-tax and after-tax results:

	Pre-Tax Results		After-Tax Results	
Interest Income	$20,000		$10,000	
Gain on redemption	20,000	$40,000	15,000	$25,000
Less: Interest paid	36,000		18,000	
Commissions	250	36,250	188	18,188
Net Gain		$ 3,750		$ 6,812

Long-term gain and ordinary deduction can also be obtained by purchasing on margin nondividend paying stock of a corporation which plows all of the corporate profits back into the business. The average

Nondividend Paying Stock

---

[6] Rev. Rul. 68-643, C.B. 1968-2, 76

investor can deduct the interest paid on the margin and pay capital
gains tax on sale of the stock.

> *Example:* In 1970, T purchases on 50 percent margin 100 shares
> of ABC stock for $50,000. T prepays one-year interest
> and deducts the entire interest paid in 1970. In 1972,
> the stock appreciates in value to $60,000 and T sells the
> stock and pays a capital gains tax on the $10,000 gain.

OBTAIN LONG-TERM GAINS IN A DECLINING MARKET—
ACQUISITION OF A PUT IN LIEU OF SELLING SHORT

If the investor is bearish with regard to a particular stock, he should
consider the purchase of a six-month, ten-day (or longer term) Put in
lieu of selling the stock short. In the event his expectations of a falling
market are realized, he may sell the Put just prior to its expiration (or
after a six-month holding period), recognizing long-term gain. (See
below and page 54.) The investor's gain will be lower as compared
to a short sale of the stock (by the cost of the Put), but the gain will be
taxed at substantially lower rates. On the other hand, had the investor
sold the stock short, any gain on the closing of the short sale would be
short-term. (See pages 48 to 53.) If the stock should rise in price, the
investor should sell the Put prior to the six-month holding period in
order to have the loss sustained treated as short-term. (See page 54.)
His loss would be limited to the cost of the Put. However, with a short
sale, his loss could be substantially greater. In view of the fact that the
amount of funds necessary to acquire a Put may be substantially less
than the funds necessary to margin a short sale, greater economic
leverage may be obtained by acquiring a Put. The economic leverage
may be further increased through the acquisition of a "discounted Put"
(the option price of the stock is below the current market price) at a
substantially reduced cost, but with the potential profit also reduced
to the extent of the discount.

> *Example:* T expects XYZ stock selling at $30 per share to fall in
> price. T purchases a six-month, ten-day Put for $300,
> which gives him the right to sell 100 shares of XYZ stock
> at $30 during the term of the option. Assume that at
> the end of six months, XYZ stock is selling for $20. T
> would then sell the Put for approximately $1,000, realiz-
> ing a net long-term gain of $700 ($1,000 less the $300
> cost of the Put). If T had sold short 100 shares of
> XYZ stock, he would have realized approximately $1,000
> economic gain which would be treated as short-term.

If T were in the 50 percent tax bracket, the long-term gain of $700 would produce $525 in after-tax income while the short-term gain of $1,000 would produce $500 in after-tax income. If XYZ stock had instead risen to $50 at the end of the six-month period, T would sustain only a $300 short-term loss (assuming he had sold the Put just prior to the six-month holding period) as compared to a $2,000 short-term loss had he sold short 100 shares of XYZ stock. T's investment in the Put would be lower if he acquired a discounted Put, e.g., $200 for a Put on XYZ stock at $27 where the market value of the stock was $30 per share.

OBTAIN LONG-TERM GAINS ON APPRECIATED OPTIONS

Sale of a Call or Put Held for More than Six Months

Where the investor holds a Call, which has appreciated in value, for more than six months, and he does not wish to maintain an interest in the stock, the Call should be sold in order to convert the recognized gain into a long-term gain. If the Call is exercised and the underlying stock is sold within six months, the resulting gain would constitute a short-term gain. (See page 55.) Similar action should be taken with respect to a Put held for more than six months. Although the acquisition of a Put is considered a short sale for purposes of applying the short sale rules, under other tax provisions dealing with options the Put is treated as a capital asset in the hands of the investor and its sale results in long- or short-term capital gain or loss depending upon the holding period.

> *Example:* The investor on June 1, 1970 purchased a six-month, ten-day Call on 100 shares of XYZ stock at $30 per share for $400. On December 2, 1970 XYZ stock is selling at $50 per share. The investor should sell the Call in lieu of exercising it then selling the stock. The sale of the Call will produce approximately $1,600 long-term capital gain, while the sale of the stock received on exercise of the Call will result in approximately the same amount of short-term gain.

Adjustments to Put or Call Option Price— Dividends, Rights, Etc.

Where the option price of a Put or Call is to be adjusted because of any dividends, etc., the time the option is exercised may be an important consideration. For example, where an extraordinary, fully taxable dividend has been declared, the exercise of the Call after the ex-dividend date would reduce the acquisition price to the investor with a possible greater capital gain upon subsequent disposition. The dividend in this instance would be taxable to the previous holder of the stock, not the investor. Similarly, an investor should exercise a Put prior to the ex-dividend date in order to produce a greater long-term capital gain (assuming the stock was held for more than six months prior to the acquisition of the Put so as to avoid the short sales rules). If the Put is exercised after the ex-dividend date the investor receives dividend income with a corresponding downward adjustment in the selling price of the stock resulting in reduced long-term capital gain. (See discussion of Puts and Calls on pages 53 to 57.)

Example: T acquires a 30-day Call on December 1, 1970 for $200 to buy 100 shares of XYZ stock at $30 (the current market price). XYZ stock will go ex-dividend an extraordinary fully taxable dividend of $5 per share on December 15, 1970. On December 14, 1970 XYZ stock is selling at $36 per share. If T exercises the Call prior to December 15, 1970, his basis in XYZ stock will be $32 per share ($30 purchase price plus $2 per share paid for the Call). The market value of XYZ stock, assuming no further fluctuation in price, will drop to $31 per share after the stock goes ex-dividend the $5 dividend distribution. Then T will be taxed on the $5 per share dividend distribution and have a potential capital loss of $1 per share (basis of $32 less market value of $31). However, if T waited until December 15, 1970 to exercise the Call, the exercise price would be adjusted downward to $25 because of the dividend distribution. Thus T would be holding XYZ stock having a fair market value of $31 per share with a basis of $27 per share ($25 purchase price plus $2 per share paid for the Call). T would now have a potential $4 capital gain and no dividend income.

Use of a Call and a Short Sale Investors expecting a sharp and substantial, but temporary, rise in the market value of a security should consider buying a six-month, ten-day Call on the stock and, when the expected rise occurs, selling the stock short. The investor thereby safeguards the amount of profit as of the desired moment of time and also retains the possibility of realizing such profit in the form of long-term capital gains. The cost of the Call, coupled with commissions and various other expenses, makes this method attractive only if a substantial but unstable rise in the market is expected. The Call is considered a capital asset in the hands of the investor, and, if sold after a six-month holding period at a gain, will result in a long-term capital gain.

Example: Let us assume that the investor on February 1 purchases for $3 per share ($300) a six-month, ten-day Call on 100 shares of Z Corporation's stock at $20 per share. One month later, when the market value of Z stock has reached $30, the investor wants to insure his net economic gain of $7 per share ($30 market value of the stock less the cost of $20 and the cost of the Call of $3 per share). However, the investor would like to maximize the after-tax effect of the $7 gain by converting as much of the gain as possible into long-term capital gain. He therefore sells short 100 shares of Z stock at $30 per share.

Action on August 2, by the investor, with resulting tax effects, will depend upon the market value of the Z stock and may be summarized by the following chart (commissions and expenses of sale have been disregarded):

Market Price of Stock on August 2	Short-Term Gain (Loss) Per Share on Covering Short Sale	Long-Term Gain on Sale of Call (or Loss on Expiration)— Per Share	Net Economic Gain Per Share
$40	($10) short-term loss	$17 long-term gain	$ 7
30	None	7 long-term gain	7
25	5 short-term gain	2 long-term gain	7
15	15 short-term gain	(3) long-term loss (if Call expires) [7]	12

LIMIT LOSS IN VOLATILE STOCK AND RETAIN POTENTIALITY OF LONG-TERM GAIN

Acquisition of a Put Simultaneously with the Purchase of Stock

The simultaneous purchase of a Put and the underlying stock under certain circumstances (described on page 51) will prevent the Put from being treated as a short sale. This exception to the short sale rules allows the investor to limit any loss in the transaction to the cost of a Put, without sacrificing the possibility of long-term gain in the event the stock increases in value. The practical use of this transaction is limited to volatile securities which may have a substantial swing in market value in either direction.

> *Example:* T purchases 100 shares of ABC stock at $70 per share and at the same time buys a six-month, ten-day Put on

---

[7] Selling the nearly worthless Call on or before August 1 would result in a short-term loss. (See page 54.)

ABC stock at $70 for $700 ($7 per share). If the market value of the stock should fall to $30 per share, T could sell the stock for $70 by exercising the Put. Thus T's loss is limited to the cost of the Put, $700. (It would appear that T could sell the Put for $4,000, recognizing a gain of $3,300, which should be given long-term capital gains treatment, provided the Put was held for more than six months. The stock could be sold immediately prior to meeting the more than six month holding period requirement, resulting in $4,000 short-term capital loss. See page 51 for further discussion of this alternative.)

Should the stock rise substantially, for example, to $100 per share, T could sell his position, recognizing gain of $2,300 (cost of unexercised Put must be added to basis of stock) which would be given long-term gain treatment if the stock was held for more than six months. If T had sold the "worthless" Put prior to the six-month holding period, there is a possibility that the $700 paid for the Put would result in a short-term loss and that the long-term gain on the subsequent sale of the stock would be correspondingly increased.

Thus T has limited any loss on the transaction to $700, the cost of the Put, and still has potential economic gain (long-term capital gain after six months) if there is a rise in the price of ABC stock.

OBTAIN LONG-TERM GAIN ON SALE OF APPRECIATED "WHEN-ISSUED" CONTRACTS

An investor who has held "when issued" stock for more than six months should consider, where practical, the private sale of the "when issued" stock (technically the sale of a contract to buy stock when and if issued) prior to settlement date, in lieu of the receipt of the new stock and the immediate sale thereof, or selling the "when issued" stock through a Stock Exchange. Gain realized on the private sale will be long-term while the sale of the new stock received, or of the "when issued" stock through a Stock Exchange, will cause the gain to be short-term (see discussion on page 58). This is similar to the sale of a Call held for more than six months as compared to the exercise thereof and selling the stock. (See page 54.)

Example: T bought 100 shares of ABC stock "when issued" on January 15, 1970 at $30 per share. The "when issued" stock is scheduled to "go regular" on December 15, 1970. Assume that on December 1, 1970, ABC "when issued" is selling for $50 per share. If T sells the "when issued" through the Stock Exchange, which is the usual transaction, the $2,000 gain will be considered to be recognized on the settlement date, December 15, 1970, as a short-term gain, even though the "when issued" stock had been held for more than six months. If T waits until December 15, 1970 to receive the "regular" stock of ABC, and then sells the stock at $50 on the next day, his $2,000 gain will still be short-term. T should sell the *"when issued" contract* on December 1, 1970, in a private sale in which case the $2,000 gain recognized will be treated as long-term.

With respect to "when issued" stock sold short (technically entering into a contract to sell stock for a fixed price when and if issued), the investor should sell or assign the contract-right rather than close out the short position. However, in this instance, it is questionable whether long-term gain will result even though the contract was held for more than six months. (See page 58.)

PROTECT GAIN ON EXERCISE OF A STOCK OPTION

A corporate executive or employee must not dispose of stock received upon exercise of a *restricted* stock option for at least two years from the time of the grant of the option (pre-1964) nor within six months after receipt of the stock. The possibility of loss during the required holding period after exercise may be eliminated by purchasing a Put concurrently with the exercise of the option.[8] (Under a *qualified* stock option plan (post-1963) the stock must be held for three years to qualify for long-term capital gain treatment. The cost of a Put for the required three-year holding period would generally be so high as to preclude this method of protecting the gain.)

Another possible way of locking in the profit on stock acquired under a restricted or qualified stock option plan and still meet the requisite holding period, is to sell short a comparable number of shares of the stock ("short against the box"—see page 1). The stock is not deemed sold until the short sale is closed. Thus a disqualifying disposition should not take place under the stock option rules. It is suggested that a short sale should not be made until the stock is held for more than six months so as to come outside of the short sale rules denying long-term

[8] Rev. Rul. 59-242, C.B. 1959-2, 125

gain treatment (see page 49). The funds arising from such transaction may be available for use by the employee (see page 3).[9]

Officers, directors and 10 percent or more shareholders of listed corporations and other corporations required to file periodic reports with the SEC are apparently forbidden by the Securities Exchange Act of 1934 [10] to sell short the stock of their corporation or to go "short against the box" for more than a limited period.

CREATE LARGER CAPITAL GAINS—SALE OF EX-DIVIDEND STOCK "FOR CASH"

Assuming no other market fluctuations, the price of stock that goes ex-dividend is generally reduced by the amount of the dividend. The investor should sell the stock before, not after, the ex-dividend date, in order to produce greater capital gain by the amount of the dividend payment. Where the stock is sold after the ex-dividend date, but prior to the record date, the sale should be made "for cash." (See page 5.) The dividend under these circumstances belongs to the purchaser. However, the selling price of the stock is increased by the amount of the dividend and will thus result in greater capital gains to the seller.

AVOID WASH SALE RULES

Short Sale— "Short Against the Box" In order to deduct a loss on securities for tax purposes and still maintain the same long position, a method frequently used in the past in order to avoid the wash sale rules, was the simultaneous purchase and short sale of the same security, and 31 days thereafter, the covering of the short position with the original shares held. The expected results were a recognition of the loss, and maintenance of the same long position with the lower basis. The Treasury has issued regulations [11] which, if upheld by the courts, would prevent this method of obtaining a deduction for the loss. (See page 48.) However, a variation of this short sale transaction might still be used effectively to accomplish the same objective of deducting the loss and maintaining the same long position. (See page 44 for discussion of wash sale rules.)

---

[9] See *First American National Bank of Nashville*, 209 F. Supp. 902, for use of deferred delivery sale as a means of avoiding market risks during the requisite holding period under the stock option rules (see page 11).

See also Rev. Rul. 57-451, C.B. 1957-2, 295, for discussion of when a disposition takes place.

[10] Section 16(c)

[11] Reg. 1.1091-1 (g)

Investors sometimes avoid the wash sale provisions by replacing securities sold with securities in another corporation in the same industry. Another method frequently utilized is "doubling up" or buying an equivalent amount of the same issue, holding both lots for 31 days and then selling the original holding and recognizing the loss. This latter method has the disadvantage of tying up and risking additional capital. Of course the investor could sell the loss securities, wait 31 days and repurchase them. However, he is now without any economic interest in the securities for the 31-day period. A sale of the loss securities in January may result in greater proceeds than a sale in December if the securities are expected to drop further in value, because of tax-loss selling at the end of the year, and then recover. Tax factors alone should not affect economic decisions.

Other Methods

AVAILABLE TAX ELECTIONS

Where the fair market value of stock rights received is less than 15 percent of the value of stock, no allocation of the basis of such stock to the rights is made unless the investor so elects. If the investor intends to sell only the rights, or to exercise the rights with a view toward selling the newly acquired stock within six months, or before selling the old shares, an election to allocate the basis should be made in order to reduce the amount of gain recognized on the sale of the rights or the new shares. An election should also be made if the investor intends to sell both his old and newly acquired shares in order to maximize the long-term gains on the old shares and reduce the amount of short-term gains on the new shares. If the old shares are sold at a loss, an election should be made so as to reduce the amount of long-term losses. Where the investor intends to retain the stock acquired on exercise of the rights, there may be an advantage in not making the election if such action results in creating widely different bases which permit selective gain or loss on later sales. Where stock dividends are received, part of the basis of the old stock *must always* be allocated to the stock dividends. (See page 37 for discussion of the method of making the allocation to either dividend stock or rights.)

Allocation of Basis to Stock Rights Received

> *Example:* T owns 100 shares of X stock with a basis of $100 per share. He receives 100 rights to purchase more shares. The market value of the stock, on the first day traded ex-rights, is $180 per share and the rights are then worth $20 per right (less than 15 percent of $180). If T sells the rights at $20 each and makes no election, he

25

will recognize $2,000 of gain (long-term or short-term depending upon the length of time the 100 shares of X stock were held). However, T may elect to allocate a portion of the basis of the $100 per share of X stock to the rights. Thus $10 ($100 times $\frac{\$20}{\$200}$) of basis would be allocated to each right. The gain that is recognized on the sale of such rights will thus be reduced to $1,000.

Obligations Issued at a Discount An investor may elect in any taxable year to include in income annually the increase in the redemption value of certain noninterest bearing obligations issued at a discount, such as Series "E" savings bonds. Otherwise the entire discount element will generally result in ordinary income treatment in the year of redemption. The election is binding and applies to all such obligations owned and later acquired. All increases in value occurring in years preceding the election must be included in taxable income in the year of election. Investors such as minors or retired persons with little or no taxable income may find this election to be most advantageous.

Recognition of gain on the increased value of certain U.S. Government obligations not previously recognized as income in the years earned may be further deferred by exchanging them for other similar obligations. (See page 65.)

Example: W purchased a $100 Series "E" savings bond for $75 in June, 1965. In 1967, she elects to include the increased annual redemption value in her income. At the end of 1967, between 2½ and 3 years have passed since the issuance date so W will recognize $6.28 of interest income, which represents the full increment in value from date of purchase to the end of the year in which the election is made. (The amount of the increment depends upon the date of issuance of the savings bond and may be affected by an increase in rates of return on such bonds.) Without such election, W would recognize $25 of interest income upon redemption of the bond at initial maturity. She could, based upon past precedents, continue holding such bond without recognizing income as Congress has not permitted any U.S. savings bonds issued since 1941 to finally mature. W could exchange the Series "E" bond for certain Series "H" bonds (which pay current interest) without being required to recognize any interest income represented in the increased value of the Series "E" bond and not previously reported as income. The interest represented by the increment in

26

value would have to be reported when the Series "H" bonds were redeemed.

Taxpayers in all tax brackets generally will find it advantageous to elect to amortize premiums paid upon the acquisition of taxable bonds. The allowable deduction for amortization operates to decrease ordinary income and to reduce the basis of the securities. The alternative is the maintenance of basis and a consequent capital loss or reduction of capital gain upon redemption or sale. (See page 62 for method of computation and restrictions.)

Amortization of Bond Premiums

> *Example:* T purchases on January 21, 1970 a $5,000 10% ABC bond due January 2, 1980 for $5,500. T elects to amortize the premium of $500 over the 10-year term of the bond, thus obtaining annually a $50 ordinary deduction. Upon redemption in 1980 for $5,000, T will recognize neither gain nor loss, since the basis will have been reduced to $5,000. However, without such election, T would sustain a $500 long-term capital loss upon redemption ($5,500 cost less redemption amount of $5,000). Thus the election gives T annual deductions against ordinary income and may prevent capital loss upon subsequent sale or redemption of the bond.

UNDESIRABILITY OF LONG-TERM GAIN IN CERTAIN SITUATIONS

Normally an investor would prefer to have recognized gains on securities transactions treated as long-term and losses treated as short-term. However, where deductions exceed income, without considering long-term capital gains, the realization of short-term gains or any type of capital losses (to wipe out the long-term gains) may be more advantageous. (Short-term capital losses should, however, be avoided if there are short-term gains against which the excess ordinary deductions can be applied.) It should be noted that this situation will not be available for noncorporate investors in taxable years after 1969 unless the investor has realized more than $140,000 of long-term gains from a pre-October 10, 1969 transaction, i.e., corporate liquidation distributions pursuant to a pre-October 10, 1969 plan or sales proceeds taxed under the installment method.[12] The following example will illustrate this point (taxpayer is married and files a joint return):

---

[12] Code: 1201(b), (c), (d).

Long-term capital gain (after deducting one-half)	$200,000
Excess of deductions over other income	$(10,000)
Taxable income	$190,000
Tax—Regular computation	$104,080
Tax—Alternative computation	$100,000
Tax payable	$100,000

If either a long-term or a short-term capital gain of $10,-
000 can be taken under the facts presented above, the
short-term gain route should be utilized. There would be
no additional tax because the additional short-term gain
will be offset by the $10,000 of excess deductions. How-
ever, a $10,000 additional long-term gain will result in
an increase in tax of $2,500 since the taxpayer is already
in the alternative tax bracket (maximum of 25 percent
tax on net long-term capital gains for years before
1970).

Assume in the above example that $10,000 of short-term
gains were included in ordinary income, with the result
that an excess of deductions did not exist. Here recognition of any short-term losses should be avoided. The first
$10,000 of such losses would not reduce the tax payable
since such losses must first offset the short-term gains,
thus wasting the $10,000 excess ordinary deductions
thereby created. However, long-term losses of $10,000
would reduce the tax by $2,500.

STOCK TRANSFER TAXES

Investors should be aware that the State transfer tax paid on the sale
of stock is properly deducted as a tax and not merely as a sales expense
in computing gain or loss in the transaction. This results in larger
capital gains or smaller capital losses and an ordinary deduction. Although the tax savings may be small in amount, the amount may be-
come significant where there have been many trades resulting in long-
term gains. Treating the State transfer taxes as deductions will also
produce extra tax deductions where the investor has net capital losses
in excess of the $1,000 maximum deduction. However, the deduction
would be lost if the investor uses the standard deduction.

Example: T had 200 separate transactions in various stocks selling
above $20 (each transaction in 100 share lots) resulting
in a net long-term capital gain of $10,000, computed by
deducting New York State transfer taxes from the pro-

ceeds of sale. Approximately $1,000 of such transfer taxes would be paid and would be allowed as an ordinary tax deduction. Thus $11,000 will be given long-term capital gain treatment. If T had instead incurred a net loss of $10,000 computed in the same manner, only $1,000 would be allowed as a deduction against ordinary income. However, T should also claim a $1,000 ordinary deduction. The remaining loss of $8,000 ($10,000 less $1,000 transfer tax less $1,000 capital loss deduction) will be available as a capital loss carry-over into future years.

INTEREST ON MARGIN ACCOUNTS

Interest charged on a stock brokerage margin account is deductible by a cash-basis taxpayer in the year in which credits such as dividends, cash deposits, or proceeds from sale of securities are made to the account sufficient to absorb the interest charge.[13] Therefore a payment should be made into the margin account towards the end of December in order to assure the deduction of interest charges of that month and prior months where there have been no recent credits to the account of adequate amounts.

Investors should consider the prepayment of the next year's interest on their margin accounts in order to create additional deductions in the current year. A prepayment may be accomplished merely by mailing a check for a stated amount with a letter indicating the nature of the payment. The taxpayer should be allowed to deduct as interest expense for the current year such a payment, if it does not exceed the anticipated interest charge for the next year based upon the current debit balance in the account. The Treasury has added another requirement that the prepayment does not materially distort income.[14]

PREPAYMENT OF STATE INCOME TAXES

Where large capital gains are subject to State income tax, it may be advisable to prepay the State income tax in order to obtain the current deduction of such taxes. Otherwise, the deduction of the State income tax on the Federal income tax return for the following year may produce a much smaller benefit.

---

[13] Rev. Rul. 70-221, I.R.B. 1970-19, 9   [14] Rev. Rul. 68-643, C.B. 1968-2, 76

CONTRIBUTION OF APPRECIATED SECURITIES

Contributions after 1969 to public charities and certain private foundations of appreciated long-term securities will result in a contribution deduction (subject to a 30 percent limitation with the excess carried forward for 5 years) equal to the fair market value of the property at the time of the gift. The appreciation in value escapes taxation. An election may be made to apply the 50 percent limitation rather than the 30 percent limitation to the contribution but only 50 percent of the appreciation would be deductible. If a contribution is made to a private foundation, other than to an operating foundation or one which passes through all of its contributions to a qualified charity within 2½ months of the following year, only half the appreciation is deductible (subject to a 20 percent limitation).[15] Taxpayers who normally make charitable donations each year should still consider giving appreciated securities or sell securities to the charity at a discount in lieu of giving cash. The cash can be used to purchase the same or similar stock and thereby obtain a high tax basis for the stock. Donations of short-term securities should be avoided since no charitable deduction will be allowed for the appreciation. Depreciated securities should also not be donated but sold to establish a tax loss. The taxpayer would then donate the proceeds if there are no appreciated long-term securities which could be contributed.

> *Example:* T normally makes $1,000 of charitable contributions each year. T has owned for more than 6 months 100 shares of ABC stock with a fair market value of $10 per share, which cost him $1 per share. T should contribute these securities to a qualified charity. In this way, $900 of appreciation would escape tax. (See below for "bargain sales" of appreciated securities.)

BARGAIN SALES OF APPRECIATED SECURITIES TO CHARITIES

A sale of appreciated securities to a qualified charity at their tax basis will also result in a contribution deduction (subject to percentage limitations) equal to the amount of appreciation. However, sales after December 19, 1969 are subject to tax. The amount of gain is determined by subtracting from the sales price a portion of the donor's basis, in the ratio of the sales price to the market value of the security.[16]

---

[15] Code: 170(b) (1) (d) and (e)   [16] Code: 1011(b)

Despite being partially taxable, a bargain sale of the security will usually result in greater after-tax dollars than an outright contribution of the security or a sale of the security followed by a cash contribution.

Example: T owns 100 shares of XYZ stock, purchased in 1968 at $40 per share. On February 1, 1970, this stock is selling at $100 per share. T, who is in the 50 percent bracket, wishes to close out his position and make a charitable contribution of $6,000. A sale would produce a $6,000 long-term gain and a tax of $1,500. His after-tax proceeds will be $8,500 ($10,000 selling amount less $1,500 in taxes). After donating $6,000 to charity and thereby reducing his tax by $3,000, he will retain $5,500 after taxes. However, if T sells the 100 shares to a qualified charity for his cost of $4,000, he would be entitled to a $6,000 charitable deduction which would reduce his income taxes by $3,000. A $600 tax would be paid on the bargain sale (25 percent of $4,000 sales price less allocated basis of $1,600). Thus, T's after-tax proceeds would be $6,400 ($4,000 selling amount plus $2,400 net savings of income taxes), or $900 more than if the security was first sold and $6,000 of cash was donated to charity. (For comparison between bargain sale and outright contribution, see page 6.)

TRANSFER OF APPRECIATED SECURITIES TO RELATIVES

High bracket taxpayers may effectively avoid the income tax on sales of appreciated securities by transferring them, at cost, to relatives, such as children, in lower tax brackets. The relatives, in turn, could sell the securities at the market value, recognizing (and paying tax on) the full appreciation. However, the investor would be subject to gift taxes on the appreciation if the amount exceeded available exemptions. Gift tax liability may or may not be important depending upon the amount of the appreciation.

Example: T owns 100 shares of ABC stock purchased November 1, 1970 at $10 per share. On December 15, 1970 this stock is selling at $30 per share. If T, who is in the 50 percent bracket, sells such securities for full value, he will recognize $2,000 of short-term capital gain and pay a tax of $1,000. However, T could sell the 100 shares to his son for $1,000 and make a gift of the balance of the value. If there were no other gifts to his son during the year, there would be no gift tax on this transfer. Assuming the son is in the 19 percent tax bracket, he would pay only

$380 of income taxes on the $2,000 short-term capital gain recognized by him upon the sale of the stock, as compared to $1,000 of tax that would have been paid by the father.

If the relative sells the securities as soon as he receives them, the Treasury may attempt to impute the gain to the high-bracket taxpayer, on the theory that the relative acted as his agent in making the sale. Therefore, it is helpful to be able to show that the relative acted as a free agent in his own behalf. This is usually easier to show in the case of an adult relative, and more difficult if the transfer is made to a minor for whom the high-bracket taxpayer is guardian.

TRANSFER OF INCOME FROM SECURITIES TO RELATIVES

A high-bracket investor who is currently providing for the needs of an elderly or indigent relative or is saving for the future needs of the younger members of the family should consider setting up ten-year support trusts.[17] A taxpayer in the 50 percent tax bracket must earn $4,000 in order to give his needy relative $2,000. By placing securities in trust for at least a 10-year period with the income distributed annually, the trust income would be taxed to the trust beneficiary and not to the grantor. As a result of the beneficiary's personal exemption and standard deduction, plus $100 dividend received exclusion, more than $1,800 can be received by the beneficiary free of tax. Any additional income will be taxed at the lowest tax brackets. Alternatively, an investor can avoid the expense of creating a support trust by taking advantage of the current high yields on tax-exempt bonds. By receiving the tax-free interest and giving it to his dependent, the investor can also claim a deduction for the dependent's personal exemption and any medical expenses paid in his behalf.

Example: T, who is in the 50 percent bracket, gives his elderly mother $2,000 annually from his dividends and interest. To obtain the $2,000 after-tax amount, T must receive $4,000 of income and pay a $2,000 tax on the income. If T sets up a trust for his mother for a period of ten years or his mother's life, whichever is shorter, with the trust principal reverting to T at the end of the period, the income would be taxed to T's mother and not to T. For

---

[17] Code: 673(a)

32

years after 1972, T's mother is entitled to a personal exemption of $1,500 (over age 65) plus a standard deduction of $1,000 and a dividend exclusion of $100. Instead of paying a $2,000 tax on the income, T's mother would pay a tax of less than $100 and would have $3,900 for her personal needs. However, approximately 30 percent of the value of the securities placed in trust would be subject to gift tax.

CAPITAL GAIN OR NONTAXABLE DIVIDENDS, AND TAX-EXEMPT INTEREST

A high-bracket investor should measure the income yield on invested capital in terms of after-tax dollars earned. Consideration should be given to investments offering tax sheltered yields such as securities in certain public utilities,[18] natural resources corporations, and trusts where part of the yield is considered a return of capital.

The investor should also compare his after-tax yield on savings bond interest, industrial bond interest and other income with interest income from tax-exempt state or municipal bonds.

The tax factors are recognized in the securities market in that variations in values do exist because of different tax treatment. For example, a U.S. Government obligation selling at a discount will sell at a price which produces a lower pre-tax yield than a U.S. Government obligation selling at par. This occurs because the discount will be treated as capital gain upon subsequent retirement.

GOVERNMENT OBLIGATIONS ACCEPTABLE IN PAYMENT OF FEDERAL ESTATE TAXES

Certain U.S. Treasury bonds selling below face value are redeemable at face value in payment of Federal estate taxes. Substantial savings in estate tax may be accomplished by the purchase of these bonds by an individual with a short life expectancy.

---

[18] These tax-free dividends will disappear in many instances after June 30, 1972.
Code: 312(m)

PRINCIPLES OF TAXATION
OF SECURITIES TRANSACTIONS

INTRODUCTION

A general coverage of the income tax provisions applicable to transactions by an individual investor, on a cash basis, in publicly traded securities is given in this section. The existence of complex tax rules necessitates a limited discussion of many types of securities transactions. A review of the 1969 Tax Reform Act provisions that may have a direct or indirect effect on securities transactions also is included in this section.

General Rules for Capital Gains and Losses
All securities held by investors except short-term U.S. or other Government obligations issued at a discount, without interest, are considered capital assets.[19] Capital gains or losses are determined by taking the difference between the sales price or proceeds received and the tax basis of the security (usually cost of the security). Sales, exchanges or redemptions of publicly traded securities will, in general, result in capital gains or losses which are divided into two basic classifications: long-term and short-term. A long-term gain or loss will generally result from the sale or exchange of a security which has a holding period (see page 38) of more than six months. A shorter holding period will result in a short-term gain or loss. All long-term transactions are netted to produce a net long-term gain or loss.[20] Short-term transactions are similarly netted. Net long-term gains are reduced by net short-term losses; net short-term gains by net long-term losses.

---

[19] Code: 1221(5)   [20] Code: 1222

34

Fifty percent of the excess of net long-term gains over net short-term losses, if any,[21] is treated, in effect, as ordinary income in computing the investor's tax. The remaining 50 percent is never taxed, but is treated as a tax preference item for purposes of the 10 percent tax on tax preferences [22] and the maximum tax on earned income.[23] For years prior to 1970, the alternative tax computation limited the tax attributable to the full net long-term capital gain to a maximum of 25 percent.[24] The maximum tax on capital gains has been raised for high-bracket investors with capital gains exceeding $50,000 to 29.5 percent and 32.5 percent for excess capital gains received in 1970 and 1971, respectively. A 35 percent maximum tax will be in effect for long-term capital gains in excess of $50,000 for 1972 and succeeding years.[25] It is important to realize that most taxpayers do not benefit from the alternative tax and therefore are not affected by the change in the maximum rates, since they are not in a more than 50 percent tax bracket and thus pay a long-term capital gain tax which will be less than 25 percent and may be as low as 7 percent. Net short-term gains in excess of net long-term losses are taxed as ordinary income. Income averaging may also be used for both types of capital gains if it will result in a lesser tax. (See page 78.)

Tax on Capital Gains

A "tax surcharge" at the annual rate of 10 percent was in effect for individuals for the period April 1, 1968 to December 31, 1969. A 5 percent annual rate applies for the period January 1, 1970 to June 30, 1970 (a 2½ percent effective rate for calendar year 1970).[26] The tax surcharge applies equally to the regular income tax and the alternative capital gains tax. Therefore, the 2½ percent effective rate for 1970 will increase the alternative tax to 25.625 percent. The surcharge can be avoided by deferring gains until 1971.

Where there is a net capital loss for the year, the amount of the loss allowed as a deduction against ordinary income is limited to $1,000, or the taxable income for the year, whichever is smaller.[27] The limitation for married persons filing separate returns is $500 each.[28] Short-term capital losses, including short-term loss carryovers, are to be first

Capital Losses and Carryovers

[21] Code section 1202 allows this 50 percent deduction in arriving at adjusted gross income.
[22] Code: 57(a) (9)A
[23] Code: 1348
[24] Code: 1201(b)
[25] Code: 1201(c). Transitional rules are also provided for amounts received before 1975

from pre-October 10, 1969 installment sales and binding contracts, and from pre-October 10, 1970 corporate distributions pursuant to pre-October 10, 1969 plans of liquidation. Code: 1201(d)
[26] Code: 51
[27] Code: 1211(b)
[28] Code: 1211(b) (2)

deducted against ordinary income up to $1,000.[29] If there are no short-term losses or they total less than $1,000, then long-term losses may be deducted to the extent of the difference. For years beginning after 1969, only 50 percent of an investor's net long-term losses may be deducted from ordinary income, subject to the above-mentioned $1,000 limitation.[30] Thus, $2,000 of long-term losses must be used to obtain a $1,000 deduction. Any amount in excess of $2,000 may be carried over to succeeding years, but the disallowed half of the $2,000 will be lost.[31] Long-term losses arising in years before 1970 continue to be deductible in full subject to the $1,000 limitation.[32] Note also that long-term losses may be deducted in full against short-term gains.

Capital loss carryovers are now allowed for an unlimited period, but the losses retain their original character. Capital losses sustained after 1963 are carried over separately as long-term or short-term losses, depending upon the nature of the losses in the year sustained and are combined with the losses of the same category for the succeeding year as if they had been incurred in such succeeding year.[33] Capital losses carried over to 1964 from the prior 5 years are considered as short-term losses for 1964 and subsequent years, regardless of whether the losses were long or short-term in the year sustained.[34] Treasury regulations provide specific rules for allocating capital carryovers between husband and wife where a joint return is filed in one year and separate returns are filed in another year.[35]

BASIS OF SECURITIES

In General The investor has the burden of proof in establishing the basis of a security sold. The Treasury may be able to impose a lesser or zero basis in the event the burden is not met.[36] Thus the importance of accurate record-keeping is self evident.

Purchase The tax basis of securities acquired by purchase is ordinarily the cost of acquisition, including the commissions paid. The interest equalization tax, if applicable (see page 76), is added to the basis of the security.

---

29 Code: 1212(b) (1)
30 Code: 1211(b) (1) (c) (ii)
31 Code: 1212(b) (2) (8)
32 Code: 1212(b) (3). Apparently, the pre July 26, 1969 losses are to be applied against ordinary income before the post July 25, 1969 losses. See House Report no. 91-413 (Part 2), p. 108.

33 Code: 1212(b) (1), before amendment
34 Code: 1212(b) (2), before amendment
35 Reg. 1.1212-1(c)
36 *Eder*, 9 TCM 98 (1950); Biggs, T. C. Memo. 1968-240; see infra for special rule when property is acquired by gift.

Securities received in exchange for other securities in a corporate reorganization or other nontaxable exchange will generally take the same basis as the securities exchanged. On the other hand, if the exchange is taxable, the fair market value at such time becomes the basis of the securities.[37] Reference to published Capital Changes services will ordinarily provide the information necessary to establish basis for any publicly-held security received in an exchange or distribution.

The basis of securities received by the investor in a taxable corporate distribution is the fair market value at such time.[38]

Taxable Distribution

The general rule is that a portion of the basis of the "old" stock is allocated to the nontaxable stock dividend (or right).[39] The allocation is based upon fair market values of the stock or rights received in relation to the fair market value of the "old" stock at the time of distribution. Where a stock distribution is taxable, e.g., is treated as a cash dividend [40] or consists of stock of another corporation, the basis of the stock will be the same as the amount of the dividend income to the shareholder. Reference to published Capital Changes services will provide the necessary percentages of allocation.

Stock Dividends and Stock Rights

Where the fair market value of rights at the time of distribution is less than 15 percent of the value of the stock, no allocation is made and the basis of the rights is zero, unless the investor elects to make the allocation under the general rule.[41] The allocation *must always* be made where stock dividends are received regardless of the market value of the properties.

Securities acquired by gift (after 1920) have a basis for purposes of determining gain equal to the donor's basis. For purposes of determining loss, the fair market value of the property at the time of the gift, if less than the donor's basis, is used.[42] Thus it is possible under certain circumstances that neither gain nor loss will be recognized. Where it is impossible to determine the basis of the donor, the fair market value at the time the donor acquired the property will be the basis to the donor for purposes of determining the donee's basis.[43]

Gift

[37] Rev. Rul. 55-757, C.B. 1955-2, 557
[38] Code: 301(d); Reg. 1.301-1(h)
[39] Code: 307; Reg. 1.307-1
[40] Code: 305

[41] Code: 307(b); Reg. 1.307-2
[42] Code: 1015(a); Reg. 1.1015-1
[43] Reg. 1.1015-1(a) (3)

The donee's basis for securities received as a gift as determined under the above rules is increased by the amount of gift tax paid with respect to the gift, but not above the fair market value at the time of the gift.[44] Where the securities received as a gift are included in the donor's taxable estate, the basis of the securities to the donee is generally the value used for estate tax purposes.[45] (See page 39 for effect on holding period.)

Inheritance Securities received by inheritance take a basis equal to the value used for estate tax purposes (fair market value at date of death or if alternate valuation is elected, the value one year after death or at date of earlier disposition).[46] An heir, however, ordinarily is not bound by the valuation used for estate taxes and is allowed to use a correct valuation.[47]

Miscella-neous The basis of securities may require adjustment due to distributions treated as a return of capital,[48] undistributed capital gains of an investment company,[49] bond premium which the investor has elected (or has been required) to amortize [50] (see page 62), annual adjustment for original issue discount on bonds issued after May 27, 1969 [51] (see page 63) and stock rights and stock dividends received.[52] Reference to published Capital Changes services will generally provide the necessary information regarding distributions, etc.

HOLDING PERIOD

Introduc-tion The determination of the holding period of securities is important in order to ascertain the nature of the gain or loss on their sale. Capital assets held for more than six months will generally generate long-term gain or loss on subsequent sale, while the sale of such assets held for not more than six months will generally cause the gain or loss to be treated as short-term. The investor has the burden of proving the length of time he has held the securities.[53]

Measure-ment of Holding Period *Acquisition by Purchase:* The period of ownership is measured in terms of whole months rather than in days. This period begins on the day after acquisition and ends on the day of sale. Stock acquired on the last day of a calendar month must be held at least until the first day of the

[44] Code: 1015(d)
[45] Reg. 1.1014-6
[46] Code: 1014(a)
[47] *Ford*, 276 F. 2d 17 (ct. cls., 1960); Rev. Rul. 54-97, C.B. 19541-, 113
[48] Code: 301(c); 1016(a) (4)

[49] Code: 852(b) (3) (D) (iii)
[50] Code: 1016(a) (5)
[51] Code: 1232 (a) (3) (E)
[52] Code: 307
[53] *Taylor*, 76 F. 2d 904 (CA-2, 1935)

seventh succeeding month, in order to be held "long-term." [54] For example, stock acquired on April 30 and sold on October 31 is not considered as being held for more than six months. However, stock acquired February 27 and sold August 28 is considered as being held for more than six months.

The *trade dates* are the controlling dates. Therefore, dates of delivery and payment (which may be delayed by holidays) generally have no effect. [55]

In an exception to the usual rule, the holding period of stock received upon the exercise of stock rights includes the day of exercise (acquisition of the stock). [56] The holding period of stock acquired through the exercise of a call begins the day after the acquisition of the stock. [57]

The date payment is received (ordinarily the settlement date) on securities sold on a stock exchange will determine the year in which gain is to be recognized. [58] However, with the probable exception of a deferred delivery under New York Stock Exchange rule 64(3) (see page 11), the holding period terminates on the trade date for purposes of determining whether the transaction is long-term or short-term. [59] The trade date determines the year in which a loss on a sale of a security is deductible. [60] (See page 5 for further details.)

The holding period of securities acquired as the result of the acquisition of a "when issued" contract begins the day after the securities are actually acquired, not when the contract is purchased. [61] Where buy and sell contracts of securities trading on a "when issued" basis are not sold or exchanged prior to their maturity, but are retained until settlement date, the sale and purchase of the underlying securities take place on the settlement date, resulting in short-term gain or loss. [62]

Losses from worthless securities are deemed to have occurred on the last day of the taxable year of worthlessness. [63]

[54] Rev. Rul. 66-7, 1966-1, C.B., 188

[55] G.C.M. 21503, C.B. 1939-2, 205; I.T. 3705, C.B. 1945, 174; Rev. Rul. 66-97, C.B. 1966-1, 190

[56] Code: 1223(6); Reg. 1.1223-1(f); Rev. Rul. 56-572, C.B. 1956-2, 182

[57] *Weir*, 10 T.C. 996

[58] I.T. 3485, C.B. 1941-1, 240

[59] I.T. 3705, C.B. 1945, 174

[60] G.C.M. 21503, C.B. 1939-2, 205

[61] I.T. 3721, C.B. 1945, 164

[62] *Shanis*, 19 T.C. 641 (1953), aff'd per curiam 213 F. 2d 151 (CA-3, 1954)

[63] Code: 165(g)

Tax-Free Exchange: Stock acquired through the conversion of a convertible bond will have a holding period beginning with the holding period of the bond. Where a cash payment is necessary in the exchange, the portion of each share of stock represented by such cash payment will receive a new holding period.[64]

Illustration: Assume a convertible bond was purchased on February 1, 1970 for $100. On October 1, 1970, when the underlying stock is worth $200, the bond is converted into 1 share of stock with the payment of an additional $50. The conversion is tax-free, but the share of stock will have a split-holding period for purposes of determining long-term or short-term gain or loss. That part of the share attributable to the bond will have a basis of $100 and a holding period relating back to the purchase of the bond whereas the portion of the share attributable to cash paid on conversion will have a basis of $50 and a holding period beginning with the day following the conversion date. However, since the stock on the conversion date had a value of $200, $150 or ¾ of such value is attributable to the bond and $50 or ¼ is attributable to the $50 cash payment. On any subsequent disposition of the share, ¾ of the sales price will be attributable to the bond portion for purposes of determining the amount and the character (short- or long-term) of the gain or loss. The remaining portion will be attributed to the $50 payment as shown by the following table:

1. Sales price	200	300	160	150	60
2. Amount attributable to bond	150	225	120	112.50	45
3. Gain or loss attributable to bond	50	125	20	12.50	(55)
4. Amount attributable to $50 payment	50	75	40	37.50	15
5. Gain or loss attributable to $50 payment	0	25	(10)	(12.50)	(35)

In general, where the investor exchanges securities in a tax-free transaction, and the basis of the securities received is determined in whole or in part with reference to the basis of the securities given up, there will be a tacking on of the holding period of the property exchanged.[65]

Gifts: A donee receiving securities as a gift may tack on to his holding period the holding period of the donor, provided that upon sale of the

---

[64] Rev. Rul. 62-140, C.B. 1962-2, 181   [65] Code: 1223(1)

securities the donor's basis is required to be used, in whole or in part, in determining gain or loss on the transaction.[66] The donor's basis is always used where securities received as a gift after 1920 are sold at a gain, but if the securities are sold at a loss, the basis of the securities is the lower of the donor's basis or the fair market value at the time of the gift.[67] Where the fair market value is lower, the donee's holding period starts at the date of the gift without any tacking on of the donor's holding period.[68]

The Treasury has ruled that if stock is purchased and placed in a margin account in joint names, then there is no completed gift.[69] Under this questionable ruling, presumably all income is attributed to the donor. No gift occurs until the donee withdraws the stock or other funds from the account.

If a gift of securities is considered to have been made in contemplation of death, the securities will have as basis the value reported in the donor's estate tax return (value at date of death or alternate valuation), and the holding period will start at the *date of the gift*. There will be no tacking on of the donor's holding period because the donor's basis was not used in determining the donee's basis.[70]

Death: The holding period of securities received as an inheritance relates back to the date of death where the decedent owned the securities and from the date of purchase if acquired by the executors or trustees. The date of distribution to the beneficiary is ordinarily not significant in determining the beneficiary's holding period.[71]

Wash Sales: (See page 44.)

Stock Rights and Nontaxable Stock Dividends: Stock rights and stock dividends received in a nontaxable distribution take the same holding period as the "old" stock.[72] Thus, when stock rights are sold, the holding period of the "old" stock is "tacked on" in determining the holding period of the rights. However, securities acquired through exercise of

[66] Code: 1223(2). The donor's holding period is used even if the donee is required to pay the gift taxes. *Turner*, 410 F. 2d 952
[67] Code: 1015(a)
[68] I.T. 3453, C.B. 1941-1, 254 (declared obso-lete by Rev. Rul. 69-43, I.R.B. 1969-5, 26)
[69] Rev. Rul. 69-148, I.R.B. 1969-13, 13
[70] Rev. Rul. 59-86, C.B. 1959-1, 209
[71] *Brewster v. Gage*, 280 U.S. 327
[72] Code: 1223(5)

the rights will not take on a "tacked on" holding period. The holding period will start on the date of exercise.[73]

Short Sales: (See page 49.)

IDENTIFICATION OF SECURITIES

Importance of Identification Where an investor holds various lots of securities acquired at different times or at different prices, and sells only a part of his holdings, the proper identification of which securities are sold has great significance in determining the tax effects of the sale. Because of differences in holding periods and bases, a sale may result in either short-term or long-term gain or loss, depending upon which securities are deemed sold. Adequate record-keeping on the part of the investor will enable him to control the type and amount of gain or loss to be recognized when a portion of a position is sold.

The Treasury has provided certain guidelines, consistent with court decisions, with respect to the identification of securities sold.[74]

Rules of the Regulations *Securities Held by Brokers, Banks, etc.:* Where securities are held by a broker in a cash or margin account or by a bank or other custodian or agent, an adequate identification of the securities sold is made if the investor specifies to the broker or other agent at the time of the sale, the particular securities to be sold and written confirmation is received from the broker or other agent within a reasonable time thereafter.[75] The designated securities are treated as sold even though the broker, etc., delivers other securities to the transferee. Identification of the securities sold from the account should be by purchase date, cost or both.[76]

Securities Held by Investor: Where securities are held by the investor, the securities sold will be those represented by certificates actually delivered, even if the investor intended, or instructed the broker to sell securities from a different lot.[77] However, where a single certificate represents securities acquired at different times or at different prices, the investor will have made an adequate identification of the portion sold, if he specifies the particular lot to be sold by identifying the pur-

---

[73] Code: 1223(6); Reg. 1.1223-1(f); Rev. Rul. 56-572, C.B. 1956-2, 182
[74] Reg. 1.1012-1(c)
[75] Reg. 1.1012-1(c) (3) (i)
[76] Reg. 1.1012-1(c) (2)
[77] Reg. 1.1012-1(c) (2); *Davidson,* 305 U.S. 44 (1938)

chase date, cost or both, of the securities, and written confirmation thereof is received from the broker within a reasonable time thereafter.[78] If transfer of part of the securities represented by a single certificate is made directly to the purchaser and not to a broker, adequate identification is made where the investor maintains a written record of the particular securities which he intended to sell.[79]

First-in, First-out: Where the investor cannot "identify" the lots from which the securities are sold, he is required to apply the first-in, first-out ("FIFO") rule, so that the securities sold are deemed to be the earliest acquired. On the other hand, if delivery is made from lots held at a particular source, then the FIFO rule applies only to securities held at that source.[80] Thus, where the investor delivers stock from lots held by broker A and other lots are held by broker B, the FIFO rule will apply only to the lots held by broker A. The FIFO rule has also been applied to the transactions in "when issued" securities.[81]

For purposes of the FIFO rule, the earliest acquisition date has been interpreted to mean the earliest beginning date of a holding period for purposes of determining gain or loss.[82] Thus, although there is some conflict in this area, the acquisition date for securities received as a gift should be the first day of the holding period and not necessarily the date of gift.[83] Nontaxable stock dividends are treated as having been acquired at the time of the original stock purchase. Stock acquired through the exercise of rights is deemed acquired when the rights were exercised. If a portion of such stock is sold and there is no specific identification, the stock deemed sold is that acquired through exercise of rights received from the earliest held stock (FIFO rule).[84]

Securities Held by Trust or Estate: Where the securities are held by the fiduciary of a trust or estate (and not by a broker or other custodian), adequate identification is made if the fiduciary specifies in writing in the trust's or estate's records at the time of disposition the particular security to be sold, transferred or distributed. A distributee must get

---

[78] Rev. Rul. 61-97, CB 1961-1, 394; see also TIR No. 334, 8/17/61

[79] Reg. 1.1012-1(c) (3) (ii)

[80] Reg. 1.1012-1(c) (1)

[81] IT 3858 CB 1947-2, 71

[82] *W. A. Forrester*, 32 BTA 745 (1935); *Curtis*, 101 F. 2d 40 (1939); *Helvering v. Campbell*, 313 U.S. 15 (1941)

[83] *Richardson v. Smith*, DC, Conn. (1938), rev'd on other issues 102 F. 2d 697; contra *Hanes*, 1 TCM 634 (1943)

[84] GCM 11743, CB XII-2, 31; *Keeler*, 86 F. 2d 265 (CA-8, 1936), cert. den. 300 U.S. 673

written notification of the particular security distributed to him. The identified security is treated as sold, transferred or distributed even though other securities are in fact delivered.[85]

Reorganizations and Partial Liquidations
Identification is possible where securities are exchanged in a tax-free reorganization. One arbitrary method of identification that has been accepted is the assigning of the lowest numbered new certificate to the earliest lot purchased.[86] In a partial liquidation, the shareholder may specifically identify the shares to be redeemed or exchanged for newly issued shares; identification is not negated because the designations were recorded incorrectly on the corporation's record.[87] In absence of identification, the FIFO rule will be applied in determining gain or loss of the cancelled shares and the basis of the newly issued or remaining shares.[88] The subsequently promulgated regulations relating to identification where a single certificate represents securities acquired at different times (see page 42) may also be applicable to these transactions.

Where adequate identification is not made and securities in the same corporation are received, the courts have generally held that the first-in, first-out method must be used.[89] However, where securities of another corporation are received in a tax-free reorganization and adequate identification is not made, the cost of the securities surrendered is averaged and allocated equally among the new securities received.[90]

WASH SALES

General Rules
Where an investor sells stock or securities at a loss and within a 30-day period before or after such sale acquires substantially identical securities, the loss will be disallowed as a "wash sale." [91] (For the definition of "substantially identical" property see the discussion on page 51 of the short sales rules, to which the term also applies.)

The entering into a contract or option to acquire substantially identical securities within the 61-day period will be treated as an actual acquisition for purposes of the wash sale rules. Thus the purchase of a "Call"

---

[85] Reg. 1.1012-1(c) (4)
[86] *Ford*, 33 BTA 1229 (A)
[87] Rule 127 F. 2d 979
[88] *Allington*, 31 BTA 42
[89] *Kraus*, 88 F. 2d 616 (CA-2, 1937); cf. *Fuller*, 81 F. 2d 176 (CA-1, 1936); but cf. *Big Wolf Corp.*, 2 TC 751 (A)

[90] *Von Gunten*, 76 F. 2d 670 (1935); cf. *Bloch*, 148 F. 2d 452 and Rev. Rul. 55-355, CB 1955-1, 418
[91] Code: 1091(a)

will bring into play the wash sale rules. Only acquisitions by purchase or in a fully taxable exchange result in disallowance.[92] Therefore, receipt of securities as a gift or in a nontaxable exchange will not be considered an acquisition.

The basis of the substantially identical securities acquired within the 61-day period will, in effect, be increased by the amount of the disallowed loss.[93] The holding period of the securities sold at a loss will be tacked on to that of the newly acquired position.[94] Thus, if the old securities were held for five months and the newly acquired securities were held for more than one month, long-term gain or loss would be recognized on the sale of the new securities.

Stock Rights, Warrants and Options

The Treasury has ruled that stock warrants come within the definition of "options" to acquire, which may cause the disallowance of a loss.[95] Thus, deduction of a loss on the sale of stock, where a warrant to buy the stock is acquired within the 61-day period, will be denied because the investor has acquired an option to buy the stock.

With respect to stock rights it is arguable that the receipt of a stock right on stock held, where a sale of the underlying stock occurs within 30 days of the receipt of the right, should not bring into play the wash sale provisions, provided the right is not exercised within the 30 day period, since the investor has not "entered into an option." However, the Treasury has ruled in a related situation, that where an employee is granted a stock option under a restricted or qualified stock option plan, for purposes of the wash sale rules, he will be deemed to have entered into an option to acquire stock on the date on which the option is granted to him.[96]

The sale of an option (stock right, warrant, etc.) and the subsequent purchase of a substantially identical security must be distinguished from a sale of a stock or security followed by the purchase of an option. The wash sales rule only applies to a loss realized on a sale of a stock or security. Section 1091 and its underlying regulations are silent as to whether a warrant or other type of option constitutes a stock or security. There are conflicting rules in other tax areas as to whether these options

---

[92] Reg. 1.1091-1(f)
[93] Code: 1091(d)
[94] Code: 1223(4)

[95] Rev. Rul. 56-406, C.B. 1956-2, 523
[96] Rev. Rul. 56-452, C.B. 1956-2, 525

are a stock or security. A right to subscribe to a security is considered a security in the tax provisions affecting security dealers [97] and exchanges pursuant to SEC orders,[98] but not for purposes of corporate reorganizations.[99] Commodity futures, however, have been held to be a security for purposes of the wash sales rule.[100] The Treasury has also impliedly ruled that a warrant is a security [101] and it may take the same view with respect to other types of options.

A second consideration is whether the subsequently acquired stock or security is "substantially identical" to a stock right, warrant, call or other option. In general, the term has the same meaning as when used for purposes of short sales.[102] A call has been ruled not to be substantially identical, for purposes of the short sale rule.[103] On the other hand, a loss on sale of a warrant was disallowed on grounds that its relative value and price changes were so similar to the later acquired stock as to make the warrant a fully convertible security and therefore substantially identical.[104] This might be the case where the stock is selling above the exercise price of the warrant so that fluctuations in the stock directly affect the market value of the warrant. The ruling did not consider other factors, such as a limited life and lack of dividend rights, in deciding that a warrant was substantially identical. Bonds issued by the same governmental agency have been ruled to be not substantially identical because of different dates of issue, dates of interest payments, maturity dates or interest rates,[105] and similar considerations should apply to warrants and other options. Stock rights more closely resemble calls than warrants because of the substantial difference between market price and option price and the shorter time available for exercise of the option. Generally, these different forms of options should not be considered substantially identical to the underlying stock or security, but as stated above, under certain conditions a warrant will be treated by the Treasury as substantially identical.

Reduction of Holdings   Losses will not be disallowed where there is a bona fide sale of securities made to reduce the investor's holdings purchased in one lot, even though the sale is made within the 30 days after the securities were purchased and even though such transaction would literally come within

---

[97] Reg. 1.1236-1(c)
[98] Reg. 1.1083-1 (f)
[99] Reg. 1.351-1(a) (ii) and 1.354-1(e)
[100] *Trenton Cotton Oil*, 147 F. 2d. 33
[101] Rev. Rul. 56-406, C.B. 1956-2, 523

[102] Reg. 1.1233-1(d) (1)
[103] Rev. Rul. 58-384, C.B. 1958-2, 410
[104] Rev. Rul. 56-406, C.B. 1956-2, 523
[105] Fn. 89 *infra*.

the statutory provisions.[106] Even where the securities are purchased in two separate lots within a short period, the same rule should apply. Further clarification by the Treasury is necessary in this area.

Gain Recognized

The wash sale rules are not applicable where the stock is sold at a gain and immediately repurchased. Sales of different lots at the same time are treated separately in determining gain or loss on the shares of each lot. For example, if lot A is purchased at $20 a share and lot B at $50 a share, and all the shares are sold at $45 a share, the loss on the sale of the shares of lot B may be disallowed under the wash sales rules.[107] Prior to enactment of the provision for unlimited capital loss carry-over,[108] investors would accelerate gain in order to wipe out any capital loss carryover that was about to expire. Such action is now rarely advantageous except possibly to offset long-term losses against short-term gains.

Sales to Related Parties

The wash sale provisions do not specifically deny a loss deduction where another member of the family or other related party purchases the same security within the 61-day period.[109] However, an attempt to circumvent these rules by having the investor's wife buy back securities sold by the investor at a loss has been frustrated by the Supreme Court under another section of the Internal Revenue Code,[110] on the ground that there was an indirect sale of the stock to the wife.[111] The wife had used her own funds, but the repurchase on the open market had occurred on the same day as the sale at substantially the same price.

Where the repurchase is at a different time and price so that there is not a "direct or indirect" sale between related parties, the loss should not be disallowed even though the repurchase by a related party is within the 61-day period.[112] If a wife is using her husband's funds and acting as his agent to repurchase the stock within the 61-day period, the transaction could be attacked as not being bona fide and the loss will probably be disallowed under the wash sale rules. Similarly, if there is an "understanding" that the securities will be repurchased the loss will be disallowed.[113]

---

[106] Rev. Rul. 56-602, C.B. 1956-2, 527
[107] I.T. 1353, C.B. I-1, 150
[108] Code: 1212(b)
[109] *Norton*, 250 F. 2d 902 (CA-5, 1958)
[110] Predecessor of Code section 267; the loss would be allowed to the wife (trans-

feree) only to the extent of the recognized gain upon subsequent sale.
[111] *J. P. McWilliams*, 331 U.S. 694 (1947)
[112] *Norton*, 250 F. 2d 902 (CA-5, 1958)
[113] *Mellon*, 36 BTA 977

Effect of Short Sales The regulations [114] treat a short sale as a true sale for purposes of the wash sale rules *if* on such date, the taxpayer owned (or had a contract or option to acquire) securities identical to those sold short *and* subsequently delivered them to close the short sale. When these conditions are not met, the short sale is deemed to occur when it is closed out by delivery of the securities. The regulations are intended to preclude the avoidance of the wash sale rules by use of the *Doyle* [115] plan ("short against the box"), which consisted of making a simultaneous short sale and purchase of the securities, waiting for just over 30 days, and then delivering the certificates representing the original holding to close out the short sale. As the regulations apply only in interpreting the wash rules, they do not change the rules applicable to short sales generally. Therefore, the technique of going short against the box to postpone the recognition of gain would not be affected. (See page 1.)

Avoidance of Wash Sale Rules See page 24 for discussion of ways of avoiding the wash sale rules. According to the Treasury, a contract for deferred delivery (see page 11) will not be a means of circumventing the wash sale rules. [116]

SHORT SALES

Definition A short sale of securities may be defined as a contract for the sale and delivery of securities the seller does not own or does not intend to make available for delivery on the sale. The securities are usually borrowed for delivery to the buyer. Such sale may be ultimately covered by the purchase of the securities in the market or by the delivery of securities already owned but not delivered to the buyer at the time of sale. [117]

Taxable Event The taxable event occurs only when the securities are delivered to close the short sale. [118] This rule is applicable whether gain or loss is realized on the sale. [119]

Statutory Rules Arbitrary statutory rules have been established with respect to "substantially identical property" in order to prevent use of short sales to convert short-term gains into long-term gains or to create artificial long-term gains and short-term losses. "Property" for this purpose includes only stock and securities including those dealt in a "when issued" basis,

---

[114] Reg. 1.1091-1 (g) and 1.1233-1 (a) (5)
[115] *Doyle*, 286 F. 2d 654 (CA-7, 1961)
[116] Rev. Rul. 59-418, C.B. 1959-2, 184
[117] *Provost*, 269 U.S. 443 (1926)
[118] Reg. 1.1233-1(a)
[119] *Hendricks*, 51 TC 235, aff'd C.A.-4, 3/4/70

48

and commodity futures which are capital assets in the hands of the taxpayer.[120] The meaning of "substantially identical property" is discussed *infra*.

The rules may be summarized as follows:

Rule 1: If property substantially identical to that sold short has been held by the taxpayer (or his spouse) [121] on the date of the short sale for not more than six months or is acquired by him after the short sale but before the closing thereof, then

   A. any *gain* on the closing of such short sale shall be considered as a short-term gain (even if property held for more than six months is used to close the short sale) ; [122] and

   B. the *holding period* of such substantially identical property becomes "tainted" and is considered to begin on the date of the closing of the short sale, or on the date of a sale, gift or other disposition of the property, if earlier.[123] The "tainting" of the holding period will apply to only an equal quantity of substantially identical property in the chronological order of its acquisition. This rule does not apply to any excess over the quantity sold short.

Rule 2: If substantially identical property has been held by the taxpayer (or his spouse) for more than six months at the time the short sale was made, any *loss* on closing the short sale is considered a long-term loss even if the property delivered to close the short sale was held for not more than six months.[124]

Where the taxpayer holds both short-term and long-term positions in securities substantially identical to the securities sold short, all the above rules will be applicable.

Illustration: Investor T purchases one share of X stock on February 1 for $10 and an additional share on April 1 for $20. T sells short one

---

[120] Code: 1233(e) (2) (A)
[121] Code: 1233(e) (2) (C) ; Reg. 1.1233-1 (d) (3)
[122] Code: 1233(b) (1) ; Reg. 1.1233-1(c) (2)
[123] Code: 1233(b) (2) ; Reg. 1.1233-1(c) (2)
[124] Code: 1233(d) ; Reg. 1.1233-1(c) (4).

Note that if a security was held for less than 6 months at the time of the short sale but for more than 6 months at the time the short sale was closed, any loss realized on the sale would be long-term under the regular rules. Reg. 1.1233-1(a) (3)

share of X stock on September 1 at $30. On December 1, the X stock is selling at $40. If T then delivers the one share purchased February 1, in order to close out the short sale position, the $20 gain will be treated, by application of rule 1(a), as short-term since substantially identical property (one share of stock purchased April 1) had been held "short-term" on the date of the short sale. In addition, the holding period of the one share of X stock purchased on April 1 is "tainted" and is considered, by application of rule 1(b), to begin on December 1, the date of the closing of the short sale. However, if the April 1 position was used to close the short sale, the gain of $10 would be short-term under rule 1(a), but the holding period of the February 1 position would not be affected since such stock was held for more than six months at the time of the short sale. If T closed his short position by purchasing one share of X stock on December 1 at $40, the loss of $10 would be a long-term capital loss by application of rule 2 since substantially identical property had been held at the time of the short sale for more than six months. The holding period of the April 1 position would be "tainted" and would be considered by application of rule 1(b) to begin on December 1, the date the short sale was closed.

An open question would appear to be whether the holding period "taint" rolls over to other substantially identical stock if the "tainted" stock is sold. Thus, where the investor purchases 100 shares of X stock on March 1 and 100 shares of X stock on March 3 and sells short 100 shares of X stock on May 15, the holding period of only the 100 shares purchased March 1 will be "tainted." If the March 1 stock is sold, and the short position is left open, do the short sale rules result in the March 3 stock becoming "tainted"? No further affirmative act seems to have occurred so as to bring the short sale rules into operation once again.

Options to Sell: The acquisition of an option to sell stock at a fixed price (referred to as a "Put") is considered as a short sale for purposes of rule 1 above (sale at a gain) and the exercise or failure to exercise such option is considered as a closing of the short sale.[125] However, the acquisition of a Put is *not* considered a short sale for purposes of rule 2 above (sale at a loss) and the exercise or failure to exercise such option is *not* considered as a closing of the short sale.[126]

---

[125] Code: 1233(b); Reg. 1.1233-1(c) (3)   [126] Code: 1233(d); Reg. 1.1233-1(c) (4)

In addition, rule 1 is not applicable if a Put and the stock intended to be used in exercising the Put are acquired on the same day, provided the stock is actually so used if the Put is exercised. Where the option does not specifically identify the property intended to be used in exercising the option, the taxpayer's records must, within 15 days after the acquisition of the stock, contain such identification. If the Put is not exercised, its cost is added to the basis of the stock with which it was identified.[127]

It would appear that where the market value of the stock has fallen so that the Put has increased in value, the Put could be sold and, if held for more than six months, the gain would be long-term. This should occur since the acquisition of the Put was not considered a short sale because of the exception discussed above. The stock could be sold prior to the long-term holding period in order to have the loss sustained treated as a short-term capital loss. (See example on page 21.) However, repeated sales of Puts under similar circumstances could negate the taxpayer's "intention" to exercise the Put with the designated stock. Under such circumstances, it could then be argued that the exception would not apply in the case of any Puts the taxpayer acquired. If this argument prevailed and the stock appreciated in value, the holding period would be "tainted" by Rule 1, since the acquisition of the Put would be considered as a short sale.

Substantially Identical Property

The short sale rules apply only when the investor holds other securities substantially identical to the securities sold short. The solution to the perplexing problem of what this term means is far from clear. Treasury regulations indicate that the term is to be applied according to the facts and circumstances in each case and generally is to have the same meaning as when used in the "wash sale" provisions.[128] This discussion covers the meaning of the term applicable to both the wash sale and short sale rules. Based upon Treasury rulings and court decisions, certain guidelines have been established.

Stocks and securities of one corporation, although not ordinarily considered to be substantially identical to stocks and securities of a different corporation, may be so considered if the corporations are prede-

---

127 Code: 1233(c) ; Reg. 1.1233-1(c) (3) 128 Reg. 1.1233-1(d) (1)

cessor and successor in a reorganization where their securities are exchanged.[129]

Where two corporations have agreed to a merger, subject to approval by shareholders, their securities should not be considered substantially identical in that too many contingencies exist, or may arise, which might prevent the merger. Even after approval by the stockholders, other contingencies, such as intervention by the federal government, may prevent the merger. However, if the market prices of the stocks are fluctuating proportionately to each other and stockholders' approval of the merger has been obtained, the Treasury might maintain that the stocks of the two corporations are substantially identical to each other.

"When issued" securities of a successor corporation may be substantially identical to the securities to be exchanged for them in a reorganization.[130] However, the Treasury has ruled that where a taxpayer has made a short sale of the "when issued" common stock of a corporation and at the time of the sale holds convertible preferred stock which is not substantially identical to the common, the conversion of the preferred into the common prior to the closing of the short sale does not constitute the acquisition of substantially identical stock.[131] (See page 58 for further discussion of the short sale rules as applicable to "when issued" transactions.)

Common stock is not considered identical to other classes of nonconvertible stock or bonds in the same corporation unless there are only minor differences between them. Convertible preferred stock, convertible bonds or warrants are treated as substantially identical to the securities into which they are convertible only when their relative values and price changes have been generally similar to the underlying security.[132] Thus, for example, where the conversion price for the bond is greater than the market price of the underlying security, the price of the bond will be more dependent upon its yield and security than upon the value of its conversion feature. Note, however, should the value of the underlying stock rise above the conversion price, the value of the bond would more closely reflect its conversion right and its price would fluctuate more uniformly with the underlying security. If the fluctuations in the price of the convertible bond and its underlying security

---

[129] Reg. 1.1233-1(d) (1)
[130] Reg. 1.1233-1(c) (6), example (6)
[131] Rev. Rul. 62-153, C.B. 1962-2, 186
[132] Reg. 1.1233-1(d) (1)

are not uniform, it is questionable whether the securities would be considered as substantially identical.

Bonds issued by the same governmental agency may not be substantially identical if there are different dates of issue, dates of interest payments, maturity dates, callable features or interest rates.[133]

A Call is not substantially identical to the underlying security for purposes of the short sale rules.[134]

See page 61 for a discussion of when commodity futures are considered to be "substantially identical."

For a discussion of the deductibility of dividends paid on a short sale, see page 69.

Dividends Paid on Short Sales

The short sale transaction lends itself to use in many situations where planned tax savings can be achieved. See pages 1, 11, 12, 13, 15, 20, 23, and 24.

Tax Savings Opportunities

PUTS AND CALLS—OPTIONS TO BUY AND SELL SECURITIES

Options to buy or sell securities may take various forms and serve many useful purposes. The two most common options used in connection with shares of stock are the Put and the Call. A Put may be defined as an option to sell stock (usually 100 shares) within a specified period of time at a specified price. A Call, on the other hand, is an option to buy certain stock at a fixed price within a stated period of time. Combinations of Put and Call options are called Straddles, Spreads, Strips and Straps, and the component Put or Call options may be exercised independently of each other. A Straddle is a combination of a Put and a Call both exercisable at the same market price. A Spread is similar to a Straddle, except that the Put price is usually below the market, while the Call price is above the market. A Strip represents a Put plus a Straddle, while a Strap is a Call plus a Straddle.[135]

Definitions

[133] Rev. Rul. 58-210, C.B. 1958-1, 523; Rev. Rul. 58-211, C.B. 1958-1, 529; Rev. Rul. 59-44, C.B. 1959-1, 205

[134] Rev. Rul. 58-384, C.B. 1958-2, 410

[135] These combinations are referred to as "multiple options" in Prop. Reg. 1.1234-2(b) (4). A grantor is permitted to identify which two of the options constitute a straddle. Prop. Reg. 1.1234-2(c)

Warrants and purchased stock rights are generally subject to the same tax rules as Calls. For treatment of stock rights received by a shareholder as a distribution, see page 73.

Functions of Options

The most important economic functions of Puts, Calls, etc., are either:

- to provide a means of reducing the risk of loss where an investment or speculation in stock is concerned, or
- to increase the leverage that can be employed.

They may be used as a vehicle for trading the underlying stock against the option or to protect a profit in a position. Certain tax considerations may favor the purchase and/or sale of each option (see pages 3, 10, 11, and 18 through 23). It is important that the cost of the option, all brokerage commissions and transfer taxes (in the purchase of a Call, not applicable to a Put) be considered in any economic or tax planning.

Treatment of Gain or Loss

These options are considered to be capital assets in the hands of the investor.[136] Tax treatment of such options depends upon their disposition.

Tax Effect on the Investor Who Purchases an Option

Sale of Option: If the option is sold, the difference between the cost of the option and the proceeds from the sale is treated as a capital gain or loss. The period for which the investor has held the option determines whether the capital gain or loss is short-term or long-term.[137]

Failure to Exercise Option: If an option is not exercised, it is treated as having been sold on the expiration date.[138] Therefore, a six-month, ten-day Put or Call which expires will produce a long-term capital loss. A shorter period option (six months or less) which expires will produce a short-term capital loss. Consideration should be given to the sale of the more than six-month option before the expiration of the six-month holding period, if it is expected that the option will not be exercised. This should create a short-term (rather than a long-term) capital loss. Where a Put has been acquired on the same day as the stock which is identified to be used if the Put is exercised so as to come within the exception to the short sale rules, then upon expiration of the Put, the

---

[136] Code: 1234(a)
[137] Reg. 1.1234-1(a)

[138] Code: 1234(b)

cost thereof is not treated as a capital loss, but must be added to the basis of the stock with which it has been identified.[139] (See page 51.)

Exercise of Option: If a Put or Call is exercised, the investor will treat the cost thereof as follows: the amount paid for the Call will increase the cost of the stock acquired, while the amount paid for the Put will decrease the proceeds of sale of the stock sold.[140] Upon the exercise of a Call, the holding period of the stock so acquired does not include the holding period of the Call, but starts the day after the Call is exercised. Acquisition of a Put is generally treated as a short sale for purposes of the short sale rules. For the effect on the holding period of the underlying stock, see page 39.

No gain or loss is recognized until the option is exercised or expires.

Tax Effect on the Investor Who Grants an Option

Failure of the Buyer of the Option to Exercise Option: The investor who grants an option will realize ordinary income at the time the option expires unexercised.[141]

Exercise of Option: The stock purchased by the investor upon the exercise of a Put he granted will acquire as a basis the option price paid by him, less the premium received on the writing of the Put.[142] The holding period of such acquired stock begins on the day after the date of the exercise of the option.[143]

For purposes of determining gain or loss, the proceeds from the sale of stock pursuant to the exercise of a Call granted by the investor will be increased by the amount of premium received upon the granting of the Call. If the stock was held by the investor for more than six months, any gain or loss, after including the premium on the granting of the option as part of the proceeds of sale, will be long-term.[144]

Reacquire Call at Loss: A loss realized by a grantor who terminated a Call for an amount in excess of the premiums originally received for the Call and sold the underlying stock at the same time will not be recognized where the grantor previously had purchased the stock and simultaneously sold the Call. The excess payment is added to the cost

---

[139] Code: 1233(c)
[140] Rev. Rul. 58-234, C.B. 1958-1, 279
[141] Ibid.

[142] Ibid.
[143] Cf. *Weir*, 10 TC 996
[144] Rev. Rul. 58-234, CB 1958-1, 279

of the underlying stock.[145] To illustrate, an investor purchased 100 shares of XYZ stock for $5,000 and simultaneously sold a 30-day Call on these shares for $750. Before the expiration of the 30-day period, the investor reacquired the Call at a cost of $1,000 and sold the stock for $5,500. The $500 gain realized on sale of the stock is reduced by the additional $250 paid to terminate the Call. The ruling would presumably not be applicable if the transactions were not simultaneous.

Dividends and Other Rights Paid during Period of the Option

Both Calls and Puts usually provide that the option price will be reduced by the value of any distributions (cash dividends, stock dividends, warrants, etc.) received on the stock during the life of the option. In such cases, all dividends, to the extent taxable, are includible in the gross income of the owner of the stock when its holder receives the dividend.[146] The adjustment to the sales price affects only the tax basis of the stock acquired on the exercise of the option and has no other tax effect.[147]

Straddles

The Treasury has announced that the premium received (by an investor) for writing a Straddle must be allocated based upon the market values (at the time the Straddle was written) of the Put and Call options contained therein.[148] In lieu of determining the market values of the two options, the taxpayer may elect by a statement attached to his income tax return to allocate 55 percent of the premium to the Call option and 45 percent to the Put option, provided that these ratios (or subsequently announced ratios) are used in allocating all future premiums received in writing Straddles.[149] The premium applicable to the unexpired option will be treated as short-term capital gain upon its expiration.[150] The premium allocated to the exercised portion of the Straddle will reduce the cost of stock acquired or increase the proceeds of sale of the stock sold, depending upon whether the Call or the Put

---

[145] Rev. Rul. 70-205, I.R.B. 1970-17, 13

[146] Ibid.; see generally I.T. 4007, C.B. 1950-1, 11; Rev. Rul. 56-153, CB 1956-1, 166; and Rev. Rul. 56-211, C.B. 1956-1, 155

[147] Rev. Rul. 58-234, C.B. 1958-1, 279

[148] Rev. Rul. 65-31, C.B. 1965-1, 365. It had been the practice of most taxpayers who wrote Straddles to allocate the entire premium received to the side of the option exercised. In recognition of that prevailing practice, the ruling applies only to Straddles written on or after January 26, 1965. Similar rules are contained in Prop. Reg. 1.1234-2.

[149] Rev. Proc. 65-29, C.B. 1965-2, 1023

[150] Code: 1234(c) (applies to Straddles written after January 25, 1965). The premium applicable to the unexercised portion of a Spread no matter when written, or to any unexercised part of a Strip or Strap not identified as part of a Straddle, will apparently be treated as ordinary income to the writer when the option expires. See Senate Finance Committee Report on Public Law 89-809.

portion was exercised. If both options lapse, the premiums would be taxed as ordinary income.[151]

With respect to Straddles or other combinations of Puts and Calls acquired by the investor, theoretically the exercise of one side of the contract should not affect the status of the unexercised portion. The part of the cost of the Straddle applicable to the unexercised option should be treated as a sale of that option on the expiration date. Thus if the Call is exercised, the cost of the Straddle applicable to such buy option would be added to the basis of the stock acquired, while the cost attributable to the Put would result in a capital loss upon its expiration. Many investors have in the past taken the position that the entire cost of the Straddle should be allocated to the portion exercised. However, in light of the Treasury's position with respect to the writing of a Straddle, a separate allocation apparently will be required.[152]

If the Call portion of a Straddle is exercised, the stock so acquired will not receive a holding period until the Put portion either is sold or expires, since the Put will be considered an open short sale and thus taint the holding period of the newly acquired long position. The holding period thus commences when the short sale is considered covered. It is therefore recommended that if the Put portion of a Straddle has any time remaining before its expiration date and is of no immediate value to the investor, the Put should be disposed of in order to allow the holding period of the newly acquired stock to commence.

"WHEN ISSUED" TRANSACTIONS

Nature of Transactions

When an investor buys or sells securities "when issued," he actually contracts to purchase or sell the securities "when, as and if issued," and for tax purposes there is no purchase or sale until the securities are issued.[153] An investor who buys and subsequently sells securities on a "when issued" basis is technically acquiring two contracts. When these contracts are cleared on the settlement date, the sale and exchange of the securities is deemed to take place on such date. Thus all gains or losses realized in such matching transactions are short-term.[154] When the investor holds several blocks of "old" securities, has sold at various

151 Prop. Reg. 1.1234-2(a)
152 Prop. Reg. 1.1234-2(f), example 1
153 *Walker*, 35 BTA 640(A)

154 *Shanis*, 19 T.C. 641 (1953) aff'd per curiam 213 F. 2d 151 (CA-3, 1954); IT 3721, C.B. 1945, 164

times the "new" securities on a "when issued" basis and cannot identify sales with specific acquisitions (see page 43), the gains or losses on the transactions are measured by matching the earliest "when issued" sales with the securities sold in order of their dates of acquisition.[155]

Wash Sale Rules

A loss sustained as of the settlement date of the "when issued" contracts will be disallowed if substantially identical securities are acquired within 30 days of that settlement date.[156] For this purpose, securities acquired under "when issued" contracts are deemed to be acquired on the settlement date. (See page 46 for further discussion of the wash sale rules and their inapplicability where sales are made in a bona fide reduction of holdings acquired within 30 days.)

Short Sales

A "when issued" security is considered property for purposes of the short sale rules.[157] Therefore the acquisition of a "when issued" security and the short sale of the "old" security or vice versa, where both are substantially identical, will cause the short sale rules to apply. (See page 52 for further discussion of the short sale rules.)

Holding Period of Securities Originally Purchased "When Issued"

If the actual securities are received pursuant to the "when issued" contract, the investor's holding period for the "new" securities will start from the settlement date and not when the "when issued" contract was acquired.[158] Thus a sale of the "new" securities at a gain immediately after the receipt thereof would result in short-term gain even if the "when issued" contract had been held for more than six months.

Sale of Contract

The Treasury has ruled that a sale or exchange of a "when issued" contract itself is the sale or exchange of a capital asset resulting in gain or loss.[159] Thus, it is theoretically possible to sell a contract to buy "when issued" stock which has been held for more than six months and have the gain treated as long-term.[160] According to the same ruling, an identical result could be achieved by selling a contract to sell securities "when issued."[161] Although the Treasury ruling apparently remains in effect, there is a possibility that the Treasury would contend that the

---

[155] *Haynes*, 17 T.C. 772 (A)
[156] IT 3858, C.B. 1947-2, 71; however, cf. Rev. Rul. 56-602 C.B. 1956-2, 527
[157] Reg. 1.1233-1(c) (1)
[158] IT 3721, C.B. 1945, 164; question (e) at page 173
[159] IT 3721, C.B. 1945, 164; Rev. Rul. 57-29, C.B. 1957-1, 519
[160] Ibid.
[161] Ibid.; see also *Stavisky*, 34 T.C. 140, aff'd 291 F. 2d 48 (CA-2, 1961)

subsequently enacted short sales rules (see page 52) prevent the long-term capital gain treatment.[162]

Practical Limitations: An attempt to sell a contract to buy or a contract to sell securities "when issued" through a stockbroker may be frustrated in that the stockbroker, applying the stock exchange rules, will consider the sale of a contract to buy "when issued" as an open sale of the "when issued" securities. Similarly, an attempted sale of the contract to sell securities "when issued" will be considered a purchase of the "when issued" securities. Thus two positions, one long, the other short, will remain open until the settlement date. It is possible that the transaction will never be consummated, thus causing all trades to be cancelled.[163] Perhaps the only solution therefore is a private assignment of the contracts.[164]

Payment for Release from "When Issued" Contract

In lieu of transferring all the rights under a "when issued" contract, if the investor could obtain a release from and cancellation of the contract itself by a payment to the other party, it may be contended that ordinary loss would result instead of capital loss. However, a payment to a third party to assume a "when issued" contract to sell has been held to result in capital loss.[165]

Worthlessness of "When Issued" Contract

If the transaction contemplated in a "when issued" contract, such as a reorganization, does not take place so that the "when issued" contract becomes worthless, it is believed that the cost of the contract, such as commissions, may be taken as an ordinary deduction.

COMMODITY FUTURES

Definition

A commodity future is a contract to purchase or sell a fixed amount of a commodity at a future date for a fixed price.[166] The exchange on

---

[162] See Sen. Rep. No. 2375, 81st Con., 2nd Sess. p. 87, C.B. 1950-2, 483, 545. The Treasury's failure to reflect in the regulations this committee report indicating that the assignment of a "when issued" contract is equivalent to the closing of a short sale, together with its virtual reaffirmation of I.T. 3721, Rev. Rul. 57-29, C.B. 1957-1, 519, would make it very difficult for the Treasury to deny long-term capital gain treatment. In *Stavisky*, 34 T.C. 140, aff'd 291 F. 2d 48, the Tax Court had an opportunity to discuss whether or not the short sale rules apply in this situation, but avoided the issue because the transaction took place prior to the effective date of the short sale rules. Under the facts of the case, the Court ruled a loss on the transfer of a short position in the "when issued" securities to be long-term capital loss.

[163] See *Stavisky*, 291 F. 2d 48 (CA-2, 1961)
[164] Ibid.
[165] Ibid.
[166] *Corn Products Refining Co.*, 350 U.S. 46, fn 1.

which the futures are traded specifies certain essential terms of the contract.

Types of Commodity Futures Transactions

Transactions in commodity futures generally fall into two classifications:

> (1) Hedge transactions used to insure against losses caused by fluctuations in price of a commodity, included in inventory or contracted for future delivery, to be used or sold in the course of business. Such transactions will invariably give rise to ordinary income or loss treatment and therefore are not further considered here.

> (2) Nonhedge transactions entered into for speculation or investment purposes with a view towards making a profit. Such transactions will generally generate capital gain or loss.

Tax Consequences of Nonhedge Transactions

In General: Futures contracts which are not hedges are generally treated as capital assets and gain or loss therefrom will generally be accorded capital gain or loss treatment. In the usual case, a commodity futures contract is held for not more than six months because of market fluctuations and therefore most gains and losses realized by the investor are short-term in nature. However, the sale of a "long" commodity futures contract which is held for more than six months results in long-term capital gain or loss.

Offsetting trades through the same broker in the same agricultural commodity future (e.g., wheat, eggs, corn, etc.) in the *same market* for the delivery in the *same contract period* are closed as of the moment the offsetting trade is made, pursuant to the rules of the Commodity Exchange Authority [167] and gain or loss is recognized at that time. Where the offsetting trade is made through a different broker, the transaction is not closed. Therefore, "long" and "short" positions are established and gain or loss is recognized only when the positions are covered. [168] Offsetting trades in non-agricultural commodity futures

---

[167] Commodity Exchange Authority Rules, Section 1.46(a)

[168] Reg. 1.1233-1 (d) (2) (iii). The Treasury had ruled, prior to the enactment of the short sale rules (Section 1233), that gain or loss must be recognized at the moment an offsetting trade is made in the same commodity future on the same market for delivery in the same contract period, even if the offsetting trade is made through a different broker. Mim 6243, C.B. 1948-1, 44; Mim 6789, C.B. 1952-1, 38; however cf. *Joseph Maloney*, 25 T.C. 1219. These rulings apparently have no current effect in light of the applicability of the short sale rules to commodity futures and the example given in Reg. 1.1233-1(d) (2) (iii).

(e.g., copper, zinc, etc.) may not be required to be closed by the exchange on which they are traded. Here also "long" and "short" positions are established and gain or loss is recognized only when the positions are covered.[169]

In determining the holding period of a commodity received in satisfaction of the commodity futures contract, the holding period of the commodity future will be tacked on.[170]

Short Sales: Under the short sale rules (see page 48) a commodity future requiring delivery in one calendar month is not substantially identical to another future in the same commodity requiring delivery in a different calendar month.[171] Thus, the regulations indicate that commodity futures in May and July wheat are not substantially identical and, therefore, the short sale rules are not applicable.[172] The short sale rules also do not apply to futures which trade in different markets even though they are substantially identical if offsetting transactions are entered into on the same day and both are closed on the same day.[173] Whether futures in the same commodity traded in different markets are substantially identical will depend upon the facts and circumstances. According to the regulations, historical similarity in price movements in the two markets is the primary factor to be considered.[174] An investor who has sold a commodity future short is precluded from enjoying any long-term capital gain upon closing the short sale by buying in the commodity future because of the short sale rules.[175]

Wash Sale Rules: The courts are in conflict both as to whether the wash sale provisions apply to commodity futures transactions and, if so, whether futures contracts with different delivery dates are "substantially identical" for purposes of the wash sale rules.[176] As mentioned previously, for purposes of the short sale rules the latter type of contracts are not "substantially identical." [177] (See page 44 for discussion of wash sale rules.)

[169] Ibid.
[170] Code: 1223(8)
[171] Code: 1233(e) (2) (B)
[172] Reg. 1.1233-1(d) (2) (i)
[173] Code: 1233(e) (3)
[174] Reg. 1.1233-1(d) (2) (i)
[175] Code: 1233(a) ; Sen. Rep. No. 2375, 81st Cong. 2nd Sess. p. 87 C.B. 1950-2, 483,

p. 545; cf. *Joseph Maloney*, 25 T.C. 1219 (1956)
[176] *Trenton Cotton Oil Co.*, 147 F. 2d 33; *Corn Products Refining Co.*, 16 T.C. 395, aff'd on other issues 350 U.S. 46; *Sicanoff Vegetable Oil Corp.*, 27 T.C. 1056, rev'd on other issues 251 F. 2d 764.
[177] Code: 1233(e) (2) (B)

BONDS

General Rules A bond, like stock, is generally considered to be a capital asset in the hands of an investor. The rules for stock are also applicable to bonds: such as basis, holding period requirements, wash sale rules, etc. Purchase commissions and similar expenses of acquiring bonds are included as part of the cost of acquisition; however, the amount paid on account of accrued interest is not included in the basis of the bond, but must be offset against the first payment of interest income.

Amortization of Bond Premiums *Wholly Tax-Exempt Bonds:* The investor is required to amortize the premium on wholly tax-exempt bonds for the purposes of computing basis; [178] however, no deduction for such amortization is allowable. [179] For state income tax purposes many states do not require the bond premium to be amortized if the interest income is subject to state tax.

Other Bonds: Investors who elect to amortize bond premiums upon fully taxable bonds will be allowed an amortization deduction in computing taxable income, provided the standard deduction is not used. [180] The election, which applies to all such bonds owned and is binding for subsequent years, must be made by claiming the deduction in the return for the taxable year in question. [181]

The total premium to be amortized with respect to any fully taxable bond acquired after 1957 is the excess of the basis of the bond for determining loss on a sale or exchange over the amount payable at maturity or any earlier call date, whichever produces the lower tax deduction. [182] See page 36 for determination of basis. Where a premium exists as the result of the addition to the basis of the interest equalization tax paid (see page 76) such premium is amortizable. [183] Special rules apply to premiums on bonds acquired before 1958. [184] The amortizable premium on a bond does not include that part of the premium which is attributable to the conversion features of the bond, determined as of the time of acquisition. [185] The premium attributable to the period prior

---

[178] Reg. 1.1016-5(b)
[179] Code: 171(a) (2)
[180] Code: 171(a) (1)
[181] Reg. 1.171-3
[182] Code: 171(b) (1) (B)—The premium on callable tax-exempt bonds must be amortized to the "earlier" call date determined under Reg. 1.171-2(b).

[183] See Senate Finance Committee report, P.L. 88-563, section .05(c) (3)
[184] Code: 171(b) (1) (B); Reg. 1.171-2(a) (2)
[185] Code: 171(b) (1); Reg. 1.171-2(c)

to the beginning of amortization may not be amortized, but remains part of the basis of the bond to be taken into account in determining gain or loss on disposition. Special rules apply where the bond is called before maturity and a portion of the premium has not been amortized, or where the bonds are not called on the call date.

Investors owning noninterest-bearing obligations issued at a discount and redeemable for fixed amounts increasing at stated intervals, such as Series "E" U.S. savings bonds, may elect to report each year the annual increment in value as income received.[186] Without the election, the investor would report the bunched amount of income when the bond is redeemed. The election is binding as to all such obligations owned or thereafter acquired and for all subsequent years. In the year of election, all increases in redemption value as of the beginning of the year must also be included in income.

Amortization of Bond Discount

In the case of all other types of obligations, other than corporate obligations issued after May 27, 1969, bond discount is not given any tax effect until the obligation is redeemed or otherwise disposed of. For corporate obligations issued after May 27, 1969, the original issue discount must be included in the investor's income on a ratable monthly basis over the life of the obligation.[187] A subsequent holder is required to amortize the remaining discount, less any amount paid for the obligation over the original issue price as increased by prior amortized discount. The basis of the obligation is increased by the bond discount included in income.[188]

The amount paid for a bond purchased between interest payment dates will generally include the interest earned to the date of purchase. The investor will reduce his first interest received by this amount.[189] When the bonds are sold, the portion of the proceeds attributable to interest earned to the date of the sale will be reported as interest income.[190] In practice, settlement dates are used in determining the amount of accrued interest.

Accrued Interest on Purchase or Sale

[186] Code: 454(a). This election is not available with respect to savings certificates issued by banks, savings and loans associations and similar organizations. Interest (or "dividends") on such certificates is held to be taxable when there is a right to withdraw it, even if the principal must be withdrawn at the same time.

(Rev. Rul. 66-44, I.R.B. 1966-9, 6; Rev. Rul. 66-45, I.R.B. 1966-9, 8)
[187] Code: 1232(a) (3)
[188] Code: 1232(a) (3) (E)
[189] Thompson Scenic Railway, 9 BTA 1203; Sol. Op. 46, 3 C.B. 90
[190] Reg. 1.61-7(d)

Interest Income

Interest income may be classified in two types, fully taxable and fully tax-exempt (partially tax-exempt bonds are no longer in existence). Most interest income from corporate bonds and federal bonds falls within the first classification. Interest on obligations of a state or other local authority, the District of Columbia, or a territory or possession of the United States generally is fully exempt from federal tax.[191] Interest on tax-free covenant bonds issued before 1934 by certain corporations is fully taxable, but a credit against tax liability of 2 percent of the interest is allowed to the taxpayer.[192] In determining which type of obligation gives the largest return, the comparison should be based on receipts after taxes.

Flat Bonds

Many bonds which are in default of interest or principal are traded "flat." The quoted price covers not only the principal, but gives the purchaser the right to unpaid accrued interest without any additional or separate charge. Payments of interest accrued prior to the date of purchase are treated as recovery of cost,[193] while payments attributable to interest earned after such date constitute interest income. If the payment of prepurchase date interest exceeds the basis of the bonds to the investor, the excess is taxed as proceeds of redemption, usually capital gain.[194] Where bonds are sold "flat," the portion of the proceeds attributable to the interest accrued after the date of purchase to the date of sale will be treated as interest income, not as giving rise to capital gain or loss.[195]

Retirement, Redemption and Disposition of Bonds

General Rule: The retirement of a bond will be considered as the sale or exchange of that bond resulting generally in capital gain or loss treatment. Bonds issued prior to 1955 must be with interest coupons or in registered form in order to qualify for this treatment.[196]

Bonds Originally Issued at a Discount: Gain on the sale or retirement of bonds held by the investor for more than six months and which were originally issued (after 1954) at a discount of more than ¼ percent a year is given special treatment.[197] That portion of the gain which represents the original discount element is treated as ordinary income,

---

[191] Code: 103. Certain "industrial development" bonds issued after May 1, 1968 and "arbitrage" bonds issued after October 9, 1969 are no longer tax-exempt. Code: 103(c) and (d)

[192] Code: 32(2)

[193] Reg. 1.61-7(c)

[194] *Rickaby*, 27 T.C. 886(A); Rev. Rul. 60-284, C.B. 1960-2, 464

[195] *Jaglom*, 303 F. 2d 847 (CA-2, 1962); *Langston*, 308 F. 2d 729 (CA-8, 1962)

[196] Code: 1232(a) (1)

[197] Code: 1232(a) (2)

with excess gain, if any, given capital gain treatment. In the case of convertible bonds, the issue price is not reduced by the value of the conversion feature in determining original issue discount.[198] Where bonds are issued with detachable warrants, however, a portion of the issue price must be allocated to the warrants, and thus original issue discount may result.[199] Allocation of each element of the investment unit is made on the basis of relative market values. If a loss is realized on disposition of the bond, it is treated as a capital loss. For the treatment of original issue discount on obligations issued after May 27, 1969 see page 63. The original discount rule generally does not apply to tax-exempt bonds or bonds purchased at a premium. However, gain on sale of tax-exempt bonds attributable to original issue discount is treated as tax-exempt interest, while the gain attributable to market discount is taxed as capital gain.[200] Where dealers acquire a series of bonds from a governmental unit at par and sell some of the bonds to the public at a discount, the Treasury has ruled that the discount is not tax-exempt.[201]

The discount on noninterest-bearing federal or municipal obligations, which are payable within one year of the date of issue, will be considered as being received when the obligation is redeemed or disposed of and the excess of proceeds over basis is taxed as ordinary income in the case of federal obligations.[202] In the case of municipal obligations, the gain attributable to original issue discount is tax exempt, while gain attributable to market discount is taxable as ordinary income.[203]

Bonds with Coupons Detached: Gain on sale of coupon bonds purchased after 1957 to the extent of the market value of detached coupons at the time of purchase of such bonds will be given ordinary income treatment.[204]

Exchange of Bonds— Deferral of Gain or Loss

Special rules permit certain exchanges of bonds for other bonds, securities or stock. Included in this classification are exchanges of bonds for bonds or stock in connection with a tax-free reorganization,[205] and conversion of bonds by their terms into stock.[206] Gain on the receipt of long-term debentures in a corporate acquisition could be deferred on sales

[198] Reg. 1.1232-3(b) (2)
[199] Code: 1232(b) (2); Reg. 1.1232-3(b) (2)
[200] Rev. Rul. 60-210, C.B. 1960-1, 38
[201] Rev. Rul. 57-49, C.B. 1957-1, 62; Rev. Rul. 60-210, C.B. 1960-1, 38, modified by Rev. Rul. 60-376, C.B. 1960-2, 38
[202] Code: 1221 (5)
[203] Rev. Rul. 60-210, C.B. 1960-1, 38; Code: 1221(5)
[204] Code: 1232(c); Reg. 1.1232-4
[205] Code: 354, 368, 371
[206] GCM 18436, C.B. 1937-1, 101

made prior to May 28, 1969 by electing the installment method for reporting gains.[207] Where convertible debentures were received in the exchange, the Treasury has informally taken the position that only the amount of the deferred gain would be taxed at the time the bonds are converted into stock. For sales contracted after May 27, 1969, marketable bonds or bonds payable on demand will be treated as cash in ascertaining whether the sale or exchange qualifies for the installment method under the 30 percent of sale price test.[208] Certain exchanges of U.S. obligations are also nontaxable.[209] The most common types of exchanges are the exchange of Series "E" bonds for other government obligations, resulting in deferment of accrued interest until ultimate redemption, and exchanges of one type of long-term government obligation for another pursuant to a special announcement. Published Capital Changes services generally provide the necessary information regarding exchanges of publicly held securities.

WORTHLESS SECURITIES

If a security becomes completely worthless during the taxable year, its cost or basis is deductible as a loss from the sale or exchange of a capital asset taking place on the last day of the taxable year.[210] No deduction is allowed for partial worthlessness or decline in market value until the security is sold or exchanged in a closed transaction.

Usually the deduction for a worthless stock loss is allowed in the year in which there is an identifiable event demonstrating worthlessness, such as bankruptcy of the corporation, reorganization with no provision for stockholders, cessation of business, etc. The Treasury frequently will insist that the loss was sustained in a later or earlier year than the one in which the loss was claimed on the return. A special seven-year statute of limitations for refund claims accords some additional protection to the taxpayer who reported the loss in the wrong year.[211] However, as one court has suggested, the only safe practice is to claim a loss for worthlessness in the earliest year possible and to renew the claim in subsequent years if there is any chance of its being applicable to the income for those latter years.[212]

---

[207] Code: 453
[208] Code: 453(b) (3)
[209] Code: 1037

[210] Code: 165(g)
[211] Code: 6511(d)
[212] *Young*, 123 F. 2d 597 (CA-2, 1941)

Ordinary and necessary expenses paid or incurred by an investor for the production or collection of income or for the management or conservation of his investments are deductible.[213]

In General

Items of investor's expenses which have been held deductible include investment counsel fees, statistical services, safe-deposit box rental, custodian fees, legal and accounting advisory services, office expenses, and secretary's salary.[214]

Types of Deductible Expenses

Carfare to visit broker for consultation is deductible,[215a] but not trips to a broker's office to watch the "ticker tapes." [215b] Expenses incurred in searching for new investments have been disallowed.[215c]

The Treasury has ruled that expenses incurred by stockholders in attending stockholders' meetings for the purposes of securing information on which to base future investment decisions are not deductible.[216] This questionable ruling is based on the theory that the expenses were not sufficiently related to the shareholder's investment activity so as to be deductible for income tax purposes. However, where the investor incurs reasonable expenses which are directly related to *present* investment interests, as, for example, the attendance at a stockholders' meeting in which the value of the investor's stock or the amount of the dividends payable may be affected, the deduction of such expenses should be allowed.[217] Expenses incurred in stockholders' proxy fights have been held to be deductible.[218]

No deduction is allowed for expenses incurred which are allocable to tax-exempt income.[219] Custodial fees are disallowed to the extent attributed to services performed for tax-exempt securities.[220] Expenses that are not clearly allocable to either taxable or tax-exempt income are generally apportioned on the basis of the ratio of each to the total gross income.[221] Similar rules apply to tax-exempts held in trust.[222]

Effect of Receipt of Tax-Exempt Income

[213] Code: 212
[214] Reg. 1.212-1(g)
[215a] *Henderson*, T.C. Memo. 1968-22
[215b] *Walters*, T.C. Memo. 1969-5
[215c] *Weinstein*, 420 F. 2d 700
[216] Rev. Rul. 56-511, C.B. 1956-2, 170; however, see *Godson*, 5 TCM 648 (1946); *Goldner*, 27 T.C. 455 (1956)
[217] Cf. Milner Est., 1 TCM 513
[218] *Surasky*, 325 F. 2d 191; *Graham*, 326 F. 2d 878; followed by Treasury if cost of proxy fight connected with production of income, Rev. Rul. 64-236, C.B. 1964-2, 64; however, see *Dyer*, 352 F. 2d 948
[219] Code: 265(1)
[220] *Alt*, 28 TCM 1501
[221] Rev. Rul. 63-27, C.B. 1963-1, 57
[222] Rev. Rul. 61-86, C.B. 1961-1, 41

Transfer Taxes   State and local transfer taxes paid on the sale of securities are deductible against ordinary income if the taxpayer itemizes his deductions and, therefore, should not be deducted from the selling price in computing gain or loss on the sale.[223] See page 28 for an example of the tax saving which can be achieved.

Excess investment interest expense will be subject to special tax treatment for years beginning after 1969.[224] For years beginning before 1972, the excess interest expense (in excess of passive investment income, such as dividends, interest, rents, royalties and short-term gains, less other investment expense) will be treated as a tax preference item the purposes of the 10 percent minimum tax.[225] For years after 1971, in lieu of the tax preference treatment, a limitation is placed on the amount of deductible investment interest expense.[226] The allowable amount is $25,000, plus net investment income including long-term capital gains, plus one-half of the investment interest expense in excess of the previously determined allowable amount. Any disallowed interest expense will be carried over to subsequent years subject to the interest expense limitations for such years. In addition, the 50 percent long-term capital gain deduction may not be taken to the extent the investment interest expense is allocated to the long-term capital gains.

Interest   Interest on a margin account is deductible by a cash-basis investor in the year in which credits are made to the account sufficient to absorb the interest charge.[227] No deduction is allowed for interest paid on indebtedness incurred or continued to carry tax-exempt bonds.[228] This would include a purchase of tax-exempts for cash in one brokerage account and a purchase by the same investor of taxable securities on margin in another account.[229] It is not necessary to trace the loan to the tax exempts, but merely to show a "sufficiently direct relationship." [230] For example, interest on a loan to finance business ventures is not a sufficiently direct relationship to an investment in tax-exempts. Once direct relationship is shown, the interest expense will be disallowed even if it exceeds the tax-exempt income.[231]

---

[223] Code: 164(a); Rev. Rul. 65-313, C.B. 1965-2, 47
[224] Pro rata rules apply for fiscal years ending in 1970.
[225] Code: 57(a) (1)
[226] Code: 163(d)
[227] Rev. Rul. 70-221, I.R.B. 1970-19, 9

[228] Code: 265(2); *Illinois Terminal Railroad Co.*, 375 F. 2d 1016; *Wisconsin Cheeseman, Inc.*, 388 F. 2d 420
[229] *B. H. Jacobson*, 28 T.C. 579 (Acq.)
[230] *Wisconsin Cheeseman*, supra; *Ball*, 54 T.C. No. 114
[231] *J. S. Wynn, Jr.*, 411 F. 2d 614 (Cert. Den.)

Interest paid on genuine indebtedness without collusion between the investor and the creditor to avoid income taxes will be allowed as a deduction.[232] There should be some economic substance to the transaction apart from income tax effect.[233] Interest deductions were denied where the court found that the transaction was not a "sham" but lacked a business purpose.[234] In addition, the Treasury has reversed its prior position and now requires interest prepaid for more than 12 months after the end of the taxable year to be deferred and be deducted over the term of the loan.[235]

Amounts equivalent to ordinary cash dividends paid by investors on stock borrowed to effectuate short sales of stock are deductible as non-business expenses.[236] The Treasury has ruled that amounts paid with respect to stock dividends or liquidating dividends on stock borrowed incident to a short sale are capital expenditures and are not deductible.[237] However, an argument can be made for treating the payment of all short dividends, including stock and liquidating dividends, as an ordinary deduction, since they are merely contractual expenses incurred as a necessary cost of obtaining the borrowed stock.[238]

Dividends Paid on Short Sales

Where the sole purpose for entering into a short sale transaction is tax avoidance without any expectation of financial gain, the short dividends paid will not be allowed as a deduction on the grounds that they are not ordinary and necessary expenses paid or incurred for the production of income.[239] However, where there is a possibility of economic gain, even though the primary purpose is tax savings through the creation of capital gain and ordinary deductions, a strong argument could be made for the deductibility of the dividends paid on the short sale.

---

[232] *L. L. Stanton*, 34 T.C. 1
[233] *E. D. Goodstein*, 267 F. 2d 127; *Knetsch*, 364 U.S. 361; *Barnett*, 44 T.C. 261, aff'd 364 F. 2d 742; *Goldstein*, 364 F. 2d 734. This latter case denies deduction of prepaid interest on a "valid" indebtedness where there is no purpose for the transaction other than to obtain a tax deduction. See also *Gilbert*, 248 F. 2d 399, 411
[234] *Rothschild*, 407 F. 2d 404
[235] Rev. Rul. 68-643, C.B. 1968-2, 76
[236] I.T. 3989, C.B. 1950-1, 34; Rev. Rul. 62-42, C.B. 1962-1, 133, *Dart*, 74 F. 2d 845 (CA-4, 1935); *Wiesler*, 161 F. 2d 997 (CA-6, 1947); contra, *Levis Estate*, 127 F. 2d 796 (CA-2, 1942)

[237] Rev. Rul. 60-359, C.B. 1960-2, 104
[238] *Main Line Distributors, Inc.*, 321 F. 2d 562—disallowed deduction on other grounds. Cf. *1955 Production Exposition Inc.*, 41 T.C. 85
[239] *Hart*, 41 T.C. 131 aff'd CA-2, 11/16/64; cf. *Carl Schapiro*, 40 T.C. 34, 39. In the *Hart* case, the transactions were mere "bookkeeping" entries with no borrowing of securities, no payment of margin, lack of investment interest, price adjustments to prevent economic substance and no delivery of stock to cover the sale.

TAX-FREE EXCHANGES

Reorgan- Recognizing that normal commercial activities would be impeded if
izations every exchange of securities were subjected to income tax despite the
lack of any substantial change in the security holder's financial position,
Congress has enacted through the years many special tax provisions
exempting certain transactions from tax. The exchange of common or
preferred stock for stock of another corporation in a statutory merger
or consolidation,[240] or the exchange of common or preferred stock for
other common or preferred stock of the same corporation in a recapitali-
zation [241] falls within this class. Other exempted transactions include an
exchange by a corporation of its voting stock for stock of another corporation which it controls after exchange,[242] an exchange of bonds for
bonds (not in excess of the principal amount surrendered) or stock of
the same corporation,[243] the conversion of convertible bonds into stock
of the same corporation,[244] and, in appropriate cases, the receipt of stock
upon division of a corporation.[245] Published Capital Changes services
generally contain the information the investor needs to determine the
proper tax treatment of exchanges of publicly-held securities.

With respect to the basis and holding period of the securities acquired
in the exchange, see pages 37 and 40.

Involuntary Special provisions deferring the recognition of gain or loss are appli-
Conver- cable to investors who were compelled to surrender their securities or
sions— receive distributions from their corporations pursuant to orders issued
Govern- by the F.C.C.,[246] S.E.C.,[247] or the Board of Governors of the Federal
mental Reserve System.[248] Published Capital Changes services generally de-
Orders scribe the proper tax treatment in these situations.

Exchange Holders of appreciated marketable securities formerly were able to
Funds diversify their holdings without recognition of gain by exchanging
these securities for stock of a mutual fund which was specifically
organized for this purpose. As a result of a recent change in the law,
such exchanges made after June 30, 1967 will be treated as taxable
exchanges.[249]

---

[240] Code: 368(a) (1) (A)
[241] Code: 368(a) (1) (E)
[242] Code: 368(a) (1) (B)
[243] Code: 354; 368
[244] GCM 18436, C.B. 1937-1, 101

[245] Code: 355; 368(a) (1) (D)
[246] Code: 1071
[247] Code: 1081
[248] Code: 1101
[249] Code: 351 (a), (d)

For discussion of tax-free exchanges of government bonds, see pages 6 and 66.

SALES TO RELATED PERSONS

Sales between related parties are viewed with suspicion by the Treasury and are strictly regulated by the Internal Revenue Code.[250] Gains realized in such transactions are generally recognized for tax purposes. Losses incurred will be disallowed for tax purposes if a member of the investor's family (spouse, descendant, ancestor, or sibling) buys the securities directly from the investor or buys them indirectly on an exchange on or about the same date and at approximately the same price.[251] The losses are not offset by gains realized on other sales.[252] The disallowed loss may be used by the purchaser to the extent the purchaser sells the security at a gain.[253] Whether the wash sale provisions can be avoided by having a related person reacquire the security is discussed on page 47.

SMALL BUSINESS INVESTMENT COMPANY STOCK

A magic formula of capital gains and ordinary losses applies to sales of small business investment company stock.[254] Losses are fully deductible by any stockholder without limitation and, if in excess of the current year's income, may be carried back or forward as a business loss. Transactions with regard to SBIC stock do not have to be "netted" with one another.[255] Therefore, if a taxpayer had gains and losses in the same year on SBIC stock, the gains would be accorded capital gain treatment, while the losses would be deductible as ordinary losses. The Treasury has ruled that a loss sustained on the closing of a short sale of stock of a small business investment company is treated as a short-term loss and not as an ordinary loss.[256] The beneficial tax treatment will be denied unless there is strict compliance with the tax provisions.[257]

CURRENT DISTRIBUTIONS ON STOCK

Dividend income is not limited to periodic distributions of cash or property. Also included in the definition are stock redemptions which

Dividend Income

[250] Code: 267
[251] *J. P. McWilliams*, 331 U.S. 694
[252] *Reddington*, 131 F. 2d 1014; *Englehart*, 30 T.C. 1013
[253] Code: 267(d)
[254] Code: 1242
[255] Rev. Rul. 65-291, C.B. 1965-2, 290
[256] Rev. Rul. 63-65, C.B. 1963-1, 142
[257] *Childs*, 408 F. 2d 531

have the effect of dividends; [258] certain sales or redemptions of shares of preferred stock which were received as stock dividends on common stock; [259] stock distributions received in lieu of cash dividends; [260] distributions of stock in a corporation other than the distributing corporation; [261] cash or other property received in a reorganization which has the effect of a dividend [262] and, according to the Treasury, cash paid in lieu of fractional stock dividends unless shareholders approve sale of fractional shares on their behalf.[263] However, a distribution is a taxable dividend only to the extent it is paid out of either accumulated or current earnings and profits.[264]

Published Dividend Records indicate the tax status as well as the total amount of dividends paid annually by publicly-held corporations. The same information, with greater detail regarding distributions in property, is available in published Capital Changes services.

To compensate to a very limited extent for the double taxation of corporate income, the Code provides that the first $100 of dividends received from most domestic corporations in a taxable year is exempt from tax.[265] (The exemption is $200 if the spouse also has at least $100 of dividend income and a joint return is filed.) The dividend received credit provisions are no longer in effect,[266] but dividends received by investors who have attained age 65 are eligible for retirement income credit.[267]

Distributions in excess of the current and accumulated earnings and profits of the distributing corporation are treated as a return of capital, reducing the basis of the stock, and, after the investor has fully recovered his cost, any excess distributions are generally taxed as capital gains.[268]

Stock Dividends A distribution of stock of the issuing corporation is generally not taxed to the stockholders. Distributions will be taxed as ordinary dividends if the stockholders have an option to receive cash or property in place of the stock dividend; or the distribution is made in discharge of preference dividends for the current year or the preceding year.[269] With

[258] Code: 302
[259] Code: 306
[260] Code: 305
[261] *Cheley*, 131 F. 2d 1018
[262] Code: 356
[263] Rev. Rul. 69-15, I.R.B. 1969-3, 10

[264] Code: 316
[265] Code: 116
[266] Code: 34
[267] Code: 37
[268] Code: 301(c)
[269] Code: 305

respect to stock distributions in place of cash dividends, the 1969 Act has expanded these provisions to include (i) disproportionate distributions among the holders of various classes of common stock, (ii) constructive distributions where one class of common stock receives cash dividends and another class obtains an increased interest in the corporate assets and earnings and profits or an increase or decrease in the ratio in which one class of securities may be converted into another class of stock, or (iii) a disproportionate distribution of convertible preferred stock.[270] Cash received in lieu of fractional stock dividends will be treated as ordinary income.[271] However, if the investor is given an option either to buy or sell fractions, and the fractional dividends are sold, capital gain or loss treatment will follow.[272] The issuance of cash for fractional shares for convenience of the distributing corporation will not cause the stock distributions to be taxable under the new section 305 rules.[273] Distributions of stock of other corporations generally are taxable as ordinary dividends. Certain distributions of stock of other corporations may qualify as tax-free "spin-offs." [274] (For discussion of tax basis and holding period of stock received as a stock dividend, see pages 37 and 41.)

The receipt of stock rights in the issuing corporation, by itself, is not a taxable event.[275] However, distributions of stock rights will be taxed as ordinary income if the stockholders have an option to receive cash or property in place of stock rights.[276]

Stock Rights

The issuance of rights to subscribe to the issuing companies' convertible bonds is also a nontaxable distribution.[277] No income would be realized either on the acquisition or exercise of the convertible bonds.[278] The Treasury has ruled that the receipt of rights to purchase the issuing company's non-convertible bonds is taxable.[279]

---

[270] Code: 305(b) (2)-(5) and (c). The rules are complex with various transitional dates but generally will not apply before 1991 to distributions on stock outstanding on January 10, 1969.
[271] Special Ruling, Dec. 21, 1960
[272] Rev. Rul. 69-15, I.R.B. 1969-3, 10
[273] Temp. Reg. ¶13.10, T.D. 7039
[274] Code: 355
[275] Code: 305
[276] Code: 305(b)
[277] *Powel*, 27 BTA 55 (Acq.)

[278] G.C.M. 13275, C.B. XIII-2, 121
[279] G.C.M. 13414, C.B. XIII-2, 124. Note that in a private ruling concerning the recent issuance of A.T.&T. rights to acquire a unit consisting of warrants and debenture bonds of the issuing corporation, the issuance and exercise were held to be nontaxable. The ruling permitted the entire option price to be attributed to the purchase of the bond with the warrant receiving the same basis as the right.

Sale of a nontaxable stock right results in capital gain or loss. In determining such gain or loss or the basis of stock acquired upon exercise of a stock right, the basis of the "old" stock is allocated to the nontaxable right based upon the fair market value of the rights received in relation to the fair market value of the stock (including the rights) at the time of distribution.[280] Reference to a published Capital Changes service will provide the necessary percentages of allocation. However, where the fair market value of the rights at the time of distribution is less than 15 percent of the value of the stock, no allocation is made, and the basis of the rights is zero, unless the investor elects to make the allocation.[281] (See page 37.)

Stock rights received in a nontaxable distribution take on the same holding period as the stock held.[282] Thus, when the rights are sold, the holding period of the stock is "tacked-on" in determining the holding period of the rights. However, securities acquired through the exercise of the rights will not take on a "tacked-on" holding period. The holding period will start on the date of exercise.[283]

Generally, no loss is recognized as a result of the failure to exercise nontaxable rights, unless the rights were acquired for a valuable consideration (e.g., acquired by purchase). No adjustment is made to the basis of the stock with respect to which the expired rights were distributed.[284]

Distributions by a corporation of rights to acquire stock of other corporations are taxable at the time of exercise or sale and not at the time of issuance.[285] The amount that is taxable as a dividend cannot exceed the lower of the spreads between option price and fair market value of the stock purchased at the time the rights are issued and at time of exercise.[286] It would appear that the amount received upon sale of the right, in excess of the spreads, should be taxable as capital gain,[287] but the Commissioner has taken the position that such amount is taxable as ordinary income.[288] The Tax Court has rejected the Commissioner's contention that the proceeds of sales constitute ordinary

[280] Code: 307(a), Reg. 1.307-1
[281] Code: 307(b), Reg. 1.307-2
[282] Code: 1223(5)
[283] Code: 1223(5); Reg. 1.1223-1(f); Rev. Rul. 56-572, C.B. 1956-2, 182
[284] Reg. 1.307-1; Special Ruling, Dec. 4, 1946

[285] *Palmer*, 302 U.S. 63; *Choate*, 129 F. 2d 684
[286] Ibid.
[287] *Gibson*, 133 F. 2d 308
[288] GCM 25063; CB 1947-1, 45

income and not dividend income.[289] The courts are split as to whether a distribution of rights to stock of another corporation may qualify as a tax-free "spin-off" [290] resulting in no gain or loss or dividend income when the rights are exercised. Dividend income may result upon the sale of such rights.[291]

INVESTMENT CLUBS

A phenomenon in recent years has been the growth of investment clubs. Basically such a club consists of a group of investors who agree to make periodic payments to be used for such investment as one or more of the investors may determine. The income or loss is allocated among the members in proportion to their holdings. For tax purposes the club is generally treated as a partnership unless all the members elect not to be treated as a partnership.[292] It is important that the club avoid falling within the classification of an association which is taxed as a corporation.[293]

FOREIGN SECURITIES AND FOREIGN CURRENCY

Foreign Income Tax Withheld

An investor may at his option claim foreign income tax withheld on income received from a foreign investment as a deduction, or as a credit against the federal income tax.[294] The latter is normally more advantageous. In either case, the full amount of the dividend before withholding must be included in income. The special election formerly available with respect to dividends from British corporations does not apply to dividends paid after April 5, 1966.

Foreign Investment Companies

Long-term gain from the sale of a foreign investment company stock is treated as ordinary income to the extent of the investor's ratable share of the company's undistributed earnings and profits after 1962.[295] The gain will be treated as capital gain if the foreign investment company elects to distribute its income currently.[296]

---

[289] *Tobacco Products Export Corporation,* 21 T.C. 625; *Baan,* 45 T.C. 71, rev'd on other grounds 382 F. 2d 485

[290] Code: 355; see *Gordon,* 382 F. 2d 499, rev'd 391 U.S. 83 and *Baan,* 382 F. 2d 485, aff'd 391 U.S. 83. The Supreme Court did not resolve this point.

[291] See *Baan* and *Gordon, supra*

[292] Code: 761

[293] Reg. 1.761-1(a)(2)(i); Code: 7701(a)(3); Reg. 301.7701-2

[294] Code: 164(a); 33; 901 et seq.

[295] Code: 1246. Similar rules apply to gains realized by an investor who owns at least 10 percent of a foreign corporation's stock. Code: 1248

[296] Code: 1247

Interest Equalization Tax

Certain acquisitions by United States citizens, or residents, or their agents, of foreign securities or indebtedness will be subject to an interest equalization tax of up to $22\frac{1}{2}$ percent.[297] The rates are subject to modification by Presidential executive order. The tax is not imposed on foreign securities acquired by the U.S. investor from a U.S. person. This exemption is available only if the seller applies for and obtains a validation certificate from the Treasury.[298] Other exemptions from this tax include investments in certain new Canadian issues and investments in less developed country corporations. The tax cannot be avoided merely by acquiring the foreign securities through a foreign broker.

Foreign Currency Transactions

Investors in foreign currencies will realize capital gains or losses upon culmination of the transaction.[299] Foreign currency held for investment is considered a capital asset and generally is subject to the same tax rules as securities.[300] But, gain on retirement of foreign debt was held to be ordinary income.[301]

INSIDER'S SHORT-SWING PROFITS

An officer, director, or 10 percent or greater stockholder of a listed corporation or other corporation required to file annual reports with the SEC may be required to turn over to the corporation the gains realized on the sale of its stock if he sells and purchases (or purchases and sells) the stock of the corporation within a six-month period.[302] Ordinarily, the executive will realize a capital loss on repayment.[303] A Tax Court decision allowing an ordinary deduction where the payment was made solely to protect the executive's reputation was reversed on appeal.[304] The problem is particularly likely to arise where the executive is in need of funds to exercise a stock option.[305] Instead of selling his stock, he should borrow the funds, with his stock as collateral, and sell the stock after the six-month period expires. A voluntary conversion of convertible bonds or preferred stock into common stock followed by a sale of the common stock within six months of the conversion date also comes within the short-swing profits provisions.[306] Advice of counsel should be obtained in all doubtful cases.

---

[297] Code: 4911 to 4931, extended to March 31, 1971 by Public Law 91-128
[298] TIR 918, July 22, 1967
[299] I.T. 3810, C.B. 1946-2, 55
[300] Cf. *Frank C. LaGrange*, 26 T.C. 191
[301] *Gillin*, U.S. Ct. of Cl., 3/20/70
[302] Section 16(b) of the Securities Exchange Act of 1934
[303] Rev. Rul. 61-115, C.B. 1961-1, 46
[304] *Mitchell*, 52 TC 170, rev'd 6th Cir. 6/18/70
[305] Cf. *Greene v. Dietz*, 247 F. 2d 689; *Babbitt Inc. v. Lachner*, S.D.N.Y. 12/13/63
[306] *Park & Tilford, Inc. v. Schulte*, 160 F. 2d 984; *Heli-Coil Corp. v. Webster*, 222 F. Supp. 831

In addition to the regular income tax, individual taxpayers for their taxable years ending after 1969, must pay an additional tax of 10 percent on their tax preference items in excess of the sum of $30,000 ($15,000 for spouses filing separate returns) and their regular Federal income tax, including tax surcharge, for the year.[307] Included in the list of tax preference items are: [308]

1. Excess investment interest (see page 68 for details);
2. Excess accelerated depreciation on net lease personal property;
3. Excess accelerated depreciation on real property;
4. Excess of value of stock over cost on exercise of qualified or restricted stock options;
5. Excess of depletion deduction over adjusted cost as reduced by prior years' depletion;
6. One-half of long-term capital gains.

As indicated previously, the average investor will not be confronted with the 10 percent minimum tax because of the $30,000 annual exclusion. Furthermore, by careful planning an investor can avoid entirely or reduce the minimum tax by making full use of the $30,000 annual exclusion plus the regular Federal income tax for the year. For example, he can stagger long-term capital gains, so that the gains plus other preference items are within the limitations.

MAXIMUM TAX ON EARNED INCOME

The maximum tax rates for income from personal services will be 60 percent for 1971 and 50 percent thereafter.[309] These rates apply only to a portion of the earned income, in the same ratio as the taxable income bears to the adjusted gross income. The eligible earned income must be further reduced by tax preference items (including one half of long-term gains) in excess of $30,000 for the current year, or if greater, the average tax preferences in excess of $30,000 for the current year and four preceding years. Any excess earned income plus other income, such as investment income, will be taxed at the regular rates. This provision will not be available to taxpayers using income averaging. (See page 78.)

---

[307] Code: 56
[308] Code: 57

[309] Code: 1348

INCOME AVERAGING FOR CAPITAL GAINS

Investors who have substantial net capital gains in the current taxable year may realize considerable savings in income tax by electing the income averaging provisions and thereby compute their tax as though the bunched income was earned over a five-year period. Income averaging is also available with respect to most types of ordinary income.[310] However, taxpayers using income averaging cannot use the capital gains alternative tax computation (see page 35) or the maximum tax on earned income. (See page 77.)

"SHAM" TRANSACTIONS

An investor may make his investments in any legitimate manner in order to obtain the maximum tax savings, and he will not be punished for choosing the avenue that produces the lesser tax.[311] This rule does not give tax effect to mere paper transactions, where in lieu of actual purchases and sales, the alleged transactions are merely entries on the broker's books.[312] Nor can an investor have recognized for tax purposes a transaction he enters into solely for tax reasons (e.g., to obtain interest deductions in the current year) with no expectation of ever realizing a profit on the transaction.[313] Through proper planning, an investor can obtain maximum tax savings without resort to "sham" transactions.

---

[310] Code: 1301-1305
[311] *Gregory v. Helvering*, 293 U.S. 465; *Karl F. Knetsch*, 364 U.S. 361
[312] *Eli D. Goodstein*, 267 F. 2d 127; *George G. Lynch*, 273 F. 2d 867
[313] See *Kapel Goldstein*, 364 F. 2d 734; *Michael J. Ippolito*, 364 F. 2d 744; *Rothschild*, 407 F. 2d 404

APPENDIXES — INDEX OF CITATIONS

REGULATIONS

TREASURY DEPARTMENT RULINGS

General Counsel's Memoranda

Mimeograph Letters

Office Decisions—Income Tax (I. T.)

Revenue Procedure

Revenue Rulings